THE OBSERVER'S
POCKET SERIES

D1179059

THE OBSERVER'S BOOK
OF BIRDS

The Observer's Books

THE OBSERVER'S BOOK OF

BIRDS

By
S. VERE BENSON

Describing
TWO HUNDRED AND FORTY-THREE SPECIES
with 200 illustrations
100 of which are in full colour

FREDERICK WARNE & CO. LTD.
FREDERICK WARNE & CO. INC.
LONDON · NEW YORK

PREFACE

The aim of this volume is to provide an inexpensive guide to British birds.   In achieving this I am indebted firstly to Messrs. Frederick Warne & Co., Ltd. for the beautiful illustrations reproduced from Lord Lilford's work *Coloured Figures of the Birds of the British Islands*, drawn by Archibald Thorburn and other well-known bird artists; also for the permission they extended to me to use any information I might be in need of from their other publications.   Secondly, I wish to acknowledge the inspiration given by T. A. Coward in *The Birds of the British Isles and Their Eggs*, not only in preparing this little book but also in past years, when his work has been my companion and great joy in studying birds.

Bird populations, both local and world-wide, vary considerably over a period of years, and great care has been taken to keep the information as up to date as possible.   Among comparatively recent changes may be mentioned the return of the Avocet, a most beautiful and graceful wading bird, to breed very successfully in a small area of East Anglia after an absence of over a hundred years. The Little Ringed Plover, previously known only as a rare vagrant, has established itself as a summer visitor, breeding at first only in the Home Counties but spreading gradually further afield. The Collared Dove from Asia has spread westwards through Europe, eventually reaching the British Isles, where it was first reported breeding in 1955. It is now a resident in a number of different localities, breeding with obvious success. Finally, we see the attempts of the Osprey to nest once more in Scotland, where in times past it was not uncommon, and the tremendous efforts of the Royal Society for the Protection of Birds to prevent its destruction and let the public benefit by its presence through a method of organised observation.

Unfortunately, the whole picture is not so rosy as these isolated additions to our birds might lead one to hope, and many species face extinction from various causes. This is not just a national problem. Unless steps are taken with speed and thoroughness, many parts of the world will lose a large part of their wild life for ever.

Perhaps the greatest factor in this trend towards irrevocable destruction is the march of civilisation, entailing the reclamation of swamps and the destruction of natural forests and wild, untouched land with the variety of plant and insect life which these foster. There are also, however, large numbers of birds which thrive on cultivated land, and others which are attracted by buildings and gardens. Until the advent of toxic chemicals, insecticides, weed-killers and chemically treated seed, the British Isles remained a happy hunting ground for at least our more familiar birds of garden and field; but our common birds are now diminishing in numbers and our birds of prey face extinction. To lovers of unspoilt country this is a tragedy, and to bird-watchers in particular it is an almost unthinkable and intolerable loss.

As for the sea, it has been marred for several decades by the waste oil from ships. This can be a nuisance on the feet and clothing of seaside holiday-makers, but to the birds it is a relentless slow black death taking its toll of hundreds of thousands of sea-birds annually.

Efforts both national and international are being made to stop this havoc, to keep a place in the world for wild and beautiful things and to find out more about the effects of chemicals in use on the land and in gardens. It should not be forgotten that we ourselves are in considerable danger from the use of many of these.

The Royal Society for the Protection of Birds and many kindred societies are supporting this research by having the bodies of dead birds and birds eggs analysed; but this is a slow and very expensive business. The process of establishing results and getting action taken to stop the use of harmful chemicals is even slower and more difficult, and meanwhile some species may have become completely extinct. We can only support the efforts being made by various bodies concerned with conservation, not only in this country but also by the International Committee for Bird Preservation (British section) at the Natural History Museum, London, which is concerned with bird protection in other countries besides our own.

We can also, of course, play our own part in assisting bird protection, as it is obvious that careless or selfish bird-watching can harm the birds. Some people, for instance, cannot leave a bird's nest alone. They handle the eggs or young, pull away all the protective covering to take a photograph, trample down the surrounding herbage, keep the sitting bird off the eggs or young for too long until they are chilled, or make such a commotion and cause so much alarm that the birds may desert their eggs.

Some bird-watchers of this kind visit colonies of birds which nest on the ground, where the eggs and chicks are wonderfully camouflaged and extremely difficult to see, with the result that these get trampled on. Even if visitors manage to avoid this, they frequently try to take photographs, keeping the parents away for too long or leaving the deserted colony a prey to crows, gulls and other predators.

Egg collecting has gone largely out of fashion, but even now some youngsters steal eggs or interfere with chicks, and others acquire a gun and pop at everything they see flying about. Professional or experienced rare-egg collectors are also still on the prowl.

More subtly injurious and hard to condemn is the bird-watcher who has become unbalanced about bird-ringing. The ringing scheme is of scientific value and has been the means of bringing to light a great deal of valuable information about bird movements; but it should be carried out with a sense of proportion and with due regard to the birds' welfare. Not so with the ringing maniac; he must catch and ring a record number of birds, especially rarities, no matter how small, no matter how badly off course in the case of a vagrant.

When it comes to bird-ringing it is more important to achieve wise restraint than to push up records. The birds ringed at migrant-observation points are usually travelling long distances in spring and autumn and arrive hungry and in a state of semi-exhaustion. The bird-ringer finds these resting in small patches of covert, usually near the coast, and sometimes his enthusiasm drives him to such a pitch that he may be seen chasing a Goldcrest or some other minute bird (in the opinion of many people, too small for ringing) from one patch of covert to another, backwards and forwards for an hour or two without rest (not for the purpose of identification); until, in sheer bewilderment and exhaustion, the unfortunate little creature finally dashes into the net which it has been trying to avoid.

This is hardly the treatment we should recommend for shy and weary migrants resting along our shores, and when the bird is a very rare vagrant and right off course, the ring is of no scientific value at all. If therefore you are going to be a ringer, please use some moderation in the way you set about it, and when in doubt as to the wisdom of a pursuit, give the bird the benefit of the doubt.

Finally, whether you are scientifically minded or just enjoy the birds in your garden, we hope you will have as much pleasure as a bird-watcher as any who have gone before you.

S. VERE BENSON

BIRD RECOGNITION

Despite all possible aids, practice is needed in recognising birds in the open. No doubt you know a sparrow or a robin, so you can start by noting whether your unrecognised bird is larger or smaller than these. If you know a racing pigeon or any kind of ordinary grey domestic pigeon, you can measure your bird in your mind's eye by one of these. You can compare a larger bird with a duck, or even with a goose or a swan. Other important points to look for are the general colour above or below, or both, and any contrasting colours such as the white bars in the wings of a Chaffinch, or the white on the outer tail-feathers, the white rump of the Bullfinch, House Martin and Wheatear, the black caps of some of the tits and warblers, and so on.

Bullfinch, 1., and House-Martin, 2., recognised by white rumps and black tails. Chaffinch, 3., recognised by white outer tail-feathers and white wing-patches. Wheatear, 4., recognised by white rump and black and white tail-pattern.

The shape of the bird is as important as the size and colour. Is it short, or has it a long tail like a Wagtail? Has it a long thin straight bill like the mud-probing Snipe, or a long curved one like the Curlew; a short stout one like a Finch, a very short small one like a Tit, or a very slender one like an insect-eating Warbler?

It is also important to notice if it runs along the ground like a Wagtail, Plover or Wader, hops along like a Sparrow, Finch or Magpie, or spends its time almost always on the wing like swifts, swallows and martins. Perhaps it is a bird which frequents trees or creeps on a tree-trunk in the manner of a squirrel, as do the woodpeckers and the tree-creepers.

A bird's flight, too, is diagnostic. It may have a dipping undulating flight as with most small birds, or it may fly on a level course like a Starling, or skim like a Swift or Swallow.

As you become familiar with all these types of birds you will gradually train your eye to take in smaller details such as eye-stripes, eye-rings, colour of legs and bill (besides the length of these), also the exact shape of the tail and wings both in flight and at rest. If you are serious about bird-watching you will make notes on the spot as to the plumage and other characteristics. Mistakes are made by trying to remember a description at a later date. Your greatest helper will always be your ear.

I am often asked how one may learn bird songs and notes; I always find that the slow method is the best. You can get records and read descriptions, but in the long run you must really stalk your bird, if it is out of sight, and see what species is uttering the call, cry or song.

Another pointer, of course, is the kind of place in which the bird is to be found. A Skylark will not be found skulking in a hedge, or a Blackbird turning over the seaweed on the beach (unless an exceptionally long and severe freeze-up has driven it from the land).

THE CLASSIFICATION OF BIRDS

Birds, like all other animals and plants, are classified into *species* (i.e. groups whose members have the greatest mutual resemblance); *genera* (groups of species); *families* (groups of genera); and *orders* (groups of families). The actual arrangement and listing of these groups in bird books has varied in the past, but there is now a trend internationally to adopt what is called the Wetmore order of classification. This arrangement of groups of birds was suggested by Dr. Alexander Wetmore, of the United States National Museum, and it was adopted by the British Ornithologists' Union in 1952. Its main purpose is to place families which are presumed to be closely related near to one another and to place the more primitive families near the beginning of the list with the more advanced families near the end. Thus the divers (order Gaviiformes) come first and the song-birds (order Passeriformes) come last.

A list of the birds in this book arranged in the Wetmore order appears on the following pages, with the number of the page on which they appear.

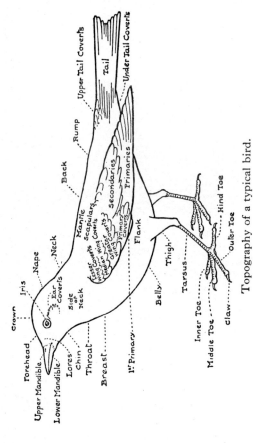

Topography of a typical bird.

Crown
Iris
Nape
Neck
Side of Neck
Ear Coverts
Forehead
Lores
Chin
Throat
Breast
Upper Mandible
Lower Mandible
Mantle
Scapulars
Lesser Coverts
Median Wing Coverts
Greater Coverts
Primary Coverts
Secondaries
Primaries
Back
Rump
Upper Tail Coverts
Tail
Under Tail Coverts
Flank
Belly
Thigh
Tarsus
Hind Toe
Outer Toe
Inner Toe
Middle Toe
Claw
1st Primary

MAGPIE

Length 18 in.

Pica pica

Resident

The Magpie is unmistakable with its glossy black and white plumage and long graduated tail. In flight the quick beat of the short black and white wings and the long tail are distinctive. Like the Jackdaw and other members of this family, it is fond of bright things, and will steal rings and trinkets.

HAUNT. General.

NEST. Of sticks, roots and mud; domed, with the entrance hole at the side; in a tree or tall bush.

EGGS. 5 to 8, pale bluish-green, speckled with brown. April.

FOOD. Small animals and birds, eggs, young birds, insects, snails, worms, fruit, grain, acorns.

NOTES. A harsh chatter.

Family *CORVIDAE*.   Crows

JAY   Length 13½ in.
Garrulus glandarius   Resident

A very handsome bird with pinkish-brown plumage, and black and white on the head and wings ; also a bright blue patch on the wings, finely barred black and white. When in flight the white rump may be noticed from a distance. It has a crest on the head which it raises and lowers at will. It is a wary bird and soon takes cover.

HAUNT. Chiefly woods and copses.

NEST. Of sticks, grass and roots ; in a bush or small tree.

EGGS. 5 to 7, pale greenish or buff, speckled with light brown. April or May.

FOOD. Small animals and birds, eggs, insect pests, grubs, snails, acorns, beech-mast, fruit.

NOTES. A harsh call repeated two or three times.

CARRION CROW
Corvus corone corone

Length 18½ in.
Resident

This is usually a solitary bird, unlike the Rook which congregates in rookeries. It is seen flying alone, or in pairs, except where feeding or roosting places attract numbers. It may also be distinguished from the adult Rook by the absence of white skin at the base of the bill. It is an all-black bird from bill to claw, as is the Raven, from which it may be told by its smaller size. In flight the wings look less ragged than those of the Rook.

HAUNT. General.

NEST. Mostly of twigs ; on a cliff ledge or high in a tree.

EGGS. 4 or 5, pale bluish-green, blotched with brown. April and May.

FOOD. Small birds and animals, eggs, carrion, grubs, insects, worms, grain, berries.

NOTES. A deep croak.

Family *CORVIDAE*.   Crows

HOODED CROW   Length 18½ in.
Corvus corone cornix   Resident and winter visitor

This and the previous bird are regarded as races of the same species.   It differs from the Carrion Crow in having an ash-grey back and underparts, and takes the place of the Carrion Crow in parts of North West Scotland and the Northern Isles, and in Ireland and the Isle of Man.

HAUNT.   It is an autumn and winter visitor, chiefly to our coasts, and a resident in Scotland, Ireland and the Isle of Man.

NEST.   Similar in material and position to the Carrion Crow's, but also may be built on the ground or in a bush.

EGGS.   4 to 6, pale bluish-green, blotched with brown.   April.

FOOD.   Carrion, scraps, small birds and animals, eggs, nestlings, shellfish, crustaceans, grubs, insects, grain.

NOTES.   A croak.

Family *CORVIDAE*. Crows

JACKDAW
Corvus monedula

Length 13 in.

Resident

This popular bird is distinguished from the Crow or Rook by its smaller size, quicker wing beats and by the grey back to its head and neck. This grey, however, is not noticeable at a distance. It is a very common bird all over the country, and may be seen singly or in flocks. It sometimes steals bright objects for no apparent reason.

HAUNT. Very general.

NEST. Of sticks, lined with grass, wool, etc. ; usually in a colony in ruins or on cliffs, or in a tree.

EGGS. 3 to 6, bluish, spotted with dark brown. April.

FOOD. Mostly grubs and insects ; also eggs, young birds and mice, and a small quantity of grain and fruit.

NOTES. " Jack " or " clack ". The alarm-note is " Caw ", very raucous and rather similar to the Rook's, but less deep.

Family *CORVIDAE*. Crows

CHOUGH
Pyrrhocorax pyrrhocorax

Length 15½ in.

Resident

Though slightly larger, this bird might be mistaken for a Jackdaw at a distance, but near by it reveals its more glossy black plumage, scarlet legs and long, curved, scarlet bill. Unlike the rest of its family, its character is as white as its plumage is black, but it has become sadly scarce. Some still breed on the west coasts of Ireland, Wales and Scotland, and a very few in extreme S. W. England.

HAUNT. Chiefly sea cliffs.

NEST. Of sticks and roots, lined with grass, wool, etc.; in a crevice in a cliff or cave.

EGGS. 3 to 6, yellowish-white, spotted with grey and brown. April or May.

FOOD. Chiefly insects.

NOTES. Usually a very loud " Chee-aw ", sometimes " chuff ".

23

Family *CORVIDAE*. Crows

RAVEN Length 25 in.

Corvus corax Resident

The Raven is not abundant in England and Wales, but is found on the west and south coasts and mountainous places. In Scotland and west Ireland it is more common. It is the largest member of the Crow family, and is easily distinguished from the Carrion Crow by its much greater size, heavier bill and wedge-shaped tail-tip. Though a solitary pair is usual, large flocks have been seen feeding or roosting in some areas.

HAUNT. Cliffs, mountains and sometimes woods.

NEST. Of sticks, lined with grass and wool ; on a cliff-ledge or on rugged rocks.

EGGS. 3 to 7, greenish, with dark brown blotches. February or March.

FOOD. Mostly carrion and small animals and birds ; also eggs, grubs, worms, grain and fruit.

NOTES. A guttural, pig-like grunt, " pruk ", or a deep croak.

ROOK
Corvus frugilegus

Length 18 in.

Resident

The Rook is more sociable than any other member of the Crow family, feeding and flying often in large numbers, and building its nest in a rookery in tree tops. The adult differs from the Carrion Crow in having a bare whitish patch round the base of the bill.

HAUNT. General where there are trees.

NEST. Of sticks and mud, lined with grass, wool and hair ; high in an elm or other tall tree. Usually there are several nests in one tree. Over forty were recorded in one tree in Cornwall.

EGGS. 3 to 6, greenish, mottled with olive-brown. Usually laid in March.

FOOD. Mostly grubs, particularly those which are harmful, such as leather-jackets and wireworms. Also eggs and a small quantity of seed.

NOTES. Chiefly " caw." or a raucous " caar ".

Family *FRINGILLIDAE.* Finches

HAWFINCH
Coccothraustes coccothraustes

Length 7 in.
Resident

A large, heavy, thickset F i n c h with a massive beak. The plumage is reddish-brown with blue-black, frilled wing - feathers and white wing-bar; and a white fringe to the tail is conspicuous in flight. The neat, small, black bib on the throat is distinctive. The female is rather paler in tone. It is a very secretive bird.

H A U N T. Rather scarce and local, but fairly widely distributed, especially in gardens.

N E S T. Of twigs, roots and fibre ; in a bush or tree.

E G G S. 3 to 6, pale buff or nearly white, with dark brown streaks and blotches. April or May.

F O O D. Berries, seeds, fruit-stones (which it cracks with its massive bill), insects, caterpillars.

N O T E S. Usually a high, sharp, " Tzik ".

GREENFINCH
Chloris chloris

Length 5¾ in.

Resident

The Green-finch, or Green Linnet, as it is often called, is slightly larger and perhaps more general in its haunts than the Linnet (Brown Linnet), and is a familiar bird of the countryside. In summer it is a soft green, varying in intensity. The yellow in the wing and tail is not very conspicuous, except when they are spread. In winter the green plumage is partly obscured by brown tips. The female is duller in colouring at all seasons.

HAUNT. General, all over the country.

NEST. Of grass, moss, twigs, hair and feathers ; in a bush or a hedge.

EGGS. 4 to 6, cream-colour, spotted with red-brown and nearly black. April–July.

FOOD. Chiefly weed-seed, also insects.

NOTES. A long-drawn, nasal " zwee ". The song is a repetition of this note interspersed with " chu, chu, chu ", and a rattling twitter.

Family *FRINGILLIDAE*. Finches

TWITE

Length 5¼ in.

Carduelis flavirostris

Resident

The Twite is the linnet of north Britain and Ireland, and replaces the true Linnet on high northern moors. It is rather slimmer than the Linnet; light brown with noticeable dark brown striations, shading to pink on the rump of the male. The light-yellow bill in winter is also a distinctive feature.

HAUNT. Heaths and moors.

NEST. Of grass, moss and wool; on the ground in heather or in a bush.

EGGS. 4 to 6, like the Linnet's, but a little smaller and sometimes bluer. May, June.

FOOD. Chiefly weed-seeds.

NOTES. Canary-like " Twite ", and other, Linnet-like flight-twittering. Song, like the Linnet's, but less varied and beautiful.

Family *FRINGILLIDAE*. Finches

LESSER REDPOLL

Carduelis flammea

Length 4¾ in.

Resident

The Redpoll is a very small, striated, brown Finch with a red forehead. It also has a soft rose-pink breast, a black chin, and a tinge of pink on the rump. The female is without the pink on the breast, but otherwise is very like the male in appearance. In the winter the plumage is less bright and has a greyer tone.

HAUNT. Among trees, and elsewhere in the country. It is more abundant in the north.

NEST. Of twigs, grass, moss and wool ; in a bush, tree or bramble-patch.

EGGS. 4 to 6, greenish-blue, speckled with brown. May and June.

FOOD. Insects and small weed-seeds.

NOTES. When feeding and flying with others it keeps up a continuous twittering. Song, uttered chiefly on the wing, " tew-tew-tew " followed by a trill.

Family *FRINGILLIDAE*.   Finches

GOLDFINCH
Carduelis carduelis

Length 4¾ in.

Resident

This is one of our smaller Finches, and is perhaps the most handsome in appearance of them all, and very dainty in its ways. Unfortunately, it has a long, sad history as a most popular cage-bird. The sexes are alike, but young birds lack the crimson, white and black on the face and head of the adult bird, though they have a similar wing-pattern.

HAUNT. Fairly general, especially in weedy waste places, where it does invaluable service by feeding on groundsel, thistle and other harmful weed seed.

NEST. Of grass, fine roots, moss, lichens, wool and thistledown ; neat and small, and may be in a bush or small tree. Orchards are a favourite site. The nest is sometimes deliberately decorated. I have seen one draped with fresh forget-me-nots.

EGGS. 4 to 6, similar to the Greenfinch's but smaller ; nearly white, speckled with purplish- and dark-brown. May.

FOOD. Weed-seeds and insects.

NOTES. A high tinkling twitter, reminiscent of Japanese wind-bells. Song, similar.

LINNET

Length 5¼ in.

Carduelis cannabina

Resident

The Linnet is one of our most lovable little songsters. It brings with it a breath of gorse - clad hillsides and summer days. In winter the male loses the crimson forehead and breast, and is brown with a greyish head. The female is duller, lacking the crimson, and her brown plumage is more striated.

HAUNT. Fairly general, chiefly in open uncultivated country, and on gorsy heaths and hills.

NEST. Of grass, rootlets, hair, wool and down ; in a bush or hedge, especially in a gorse bush.

EGGS. 4 to 6, nearly white or pale blue, with dark specks.   April–June.

FOOD. Weed-seeds and insects.

NOTES. A musical " tweet ". Little flocks twitter in flight. The song is sweet and very varied ; often almost dreamy, at other times rising to an exuberant trilling twitter. It has been likened to the Canary's, but is lower and more varied and individual.

Family *FRINGILLIDAE*. Finches

CROSSBILL   Length about 6½ in.
Loxia curvirostra   Resident and visitor

Unlike all other Finches in having the tips of its mandibles overlapping and crossing. The adult male is red with brown wings and tail. Younger birds are shaded with yellow and orange. The female is olive-green and yellow, mottled and striated with brown.

HAUNT. Mostly in woods, especially firwoods. The Continental race breeds in East Anglia while the Scottish Crossbill (*Loxia pityopsittacus scotica*), with heavier bill, breeds in the Highlands.

NEST. Of grass, moss and lichens; high in a fir-tree.

EGGS. 4 or 5, nearly white, spotted with red-brown. February, March or later.

FOOD. Tree and fruit seeds, especially the seeds in fir-cones, which it extracts.

NOTES. "Quip-quip-quip," chiefly heard from flocks in flight. Song, variable, twanging or trilling, Greenfinch-like, sometimes Great-Tit-like.

BRAMBLING　　　　　　　　　Length 5¾ in.
Fringilla montifringilla　　　Winter visitor

The Brambling is a winter visitor to this country, and may be seen with Chaffinches and other Finches searching for beech-nuts or insects. The plumage, though not so bright in the winter as in summer, is rather smart. The head of the male is glossy black, and the wings and tail brown. The wings are handsomely barred with white and chestnut, and there is chestnut on the shoulders and breast. The lower back and underparts are white. In the winter the chestnut and black plumage is partly obscured with brown tips. The female is browner.

HAUNT. Woods and fields. A favourite spot is under beech-trees, where it searches for mast.

FOOD. Insects and their larvae, mast and small seeds.

NOTES. Some are similar to those of Chaffinch, but song is a single, deep, rasping, greenfinch-like " dzweee ".

CHAFFINCH
Fringilla coelebs

Length 6 in.
Resident

The Chaffinch is one of our most familiar and cheery birds. The plumage of the male is brown above, shading to olive on the rump, and there are very conspicuous white bars on the wings. The breast is pink, and there is slate-blue on the head behind the eye and on the crown. In winter the plumage is not so bright. The female appears smaller, and is duller in colour : olive-brown with white bars on the wings.

HAUNT.   Very general, and particularly near human habitations, though not thriving in the heart of cities like the Sparrow.

NEST.   Very neat and round, of moss, lichens, wool, feathers and hair, well worked and felted together ; in a bush or the fork of a tree.

EGGS.   4 to 6, grey, tinged with pink, and with brown blotches. April, May.

FOOD.   Insects, weed-seed and beech-mast.

NOTES.   " Pink ", and a questioning " weet ". The song is a rollicking cadence, ending up with a flourish.

Family *FRINGILLIDAE.* Finches

BULLFINCH
Pyrrhula pyrrhula

Length 5¾ in.

Resident

The Bullfinch is a handsome, stout Finch with deep rose - pink b r e a s t, black head and blue-grey back. The female is duller, lacking the rosy b r e a s t. Both b i r d s h a v e noticeable white rumps.

HAUNT. Rather g e n e r a l. In gardens i t i s destructive in pecking off buds of fruit trees, but it also does good by eating injurious insects and the seeds of harmful weeds.

NEST. Of twigs, roots and hair ; in a tree or bush.

EGGS. 4 to 6, greenish-blue, spotted with red-brown, purple and black. April–June.

FOOD. Chiefly weed-seeds and berries ; also insects in summer.

NOTES. A single, low, plaintive note. There is also a low but musical song.

SISKIN   Length 4¾ in.

Carduelis spinus   Resident

The Siskin is rather similar to the Greenfinch in colouring, but it is a smaller bird. The plumage is green on the back, shading to yellowish on the rump, and the yellowish-green breast shades to white on the underparts. The crown and chin of the male are nearly black. The female is not so bright, and is striated on the head and underparts. The Siskin is a winter visitor, and a resident in parts of Scotland.

HAUNT.   Chiefly among trees, especially firs, where it searches for tree-seeds and insects.

NEST.   Of twigs, moss, grass, hair and wool or feathers ; usually on the branch of a fir-tree.

EGGS.   4 or 5, bluish-white, spotted with lilac and brown.   April to June.

FOOD.   Seeds of trees and wild plants, also insects.

NOTES.   High, musical, but querulous " tzueet ", and twittering on the wing.   Song, a sweet twitter ending in a rasping wheeze, often given in circling, butterfly-like flight with fanned tail.

Family *FRINGILLIDAE*. Finches

CIRL BUNTING

Emberiza cirlus

Length 6½ in.

Resident

The Cirl Bunting is not unlike the Yellowhammer but it has an olive-green tinge on the head and across the breast. The cheeks are lemon-yellow with a black band through the eye, and the chin and throat are black. The underparts are pale yellow striated with brown, and the back is chestnut-brown. Like the Yellowhammer the white outer tail feathers are  noticeable in flight. In winter the plumage is duller. The female lacks the black and yellow head, and is brown and much striated.

HAUNT. Open or wooded country, and hedge-rows, in south Britain, but nowhere as common as the Yellowhammer.

NEST. Of grass, moss and hair ; usually in a bush or hedge, occasionally on the ground.

EGGS. 4 to 6, like the Yellowhammer's, boldly blotched and scribbled, on a white ground. May–July.

FOOD. Insects and weed-seeds.

NOTES. Similar to the Yellowhammer's. The song is " tit tit tit tit tit tit tit tit ", all on one note, lacking the last note of the Yellowhammer's song.

YELLOWHAMMER

Emberiza citrinella

Length 6½ in.

Resident

A very familiar and handsome bird of country lanes and hedgerows. The plumage varies in brilliancy, older males being a much brighter yellow, with fewer brown striations. The female's plumage is more striated, and the head is also mottled and has, in addition, a nearly black moustache line. Young males are brown nearly all over, except for the head. In flight, when seen from behind, the Yellowhammer appears a bright brown bird, with yellow head and noticeable white outer tail feathers.

HAUNT.   General, chiefly open country and hedgerows.

NEST.   Of grass, moss and hair ; low in a bush or hedge, or on the ground.

EGGS.   3 to 5, nearly white, scribbled with dark purplish-brown, from which the bird gets its name " Scribe " May–July.

FOOD.   Mostly insects, also weed-seed.

NOTES.   " Cick ". The song is " tit, tit, tit, tit, tit, tit, *tee* ", the last note being higher, or occasionally lower, than the rest of the song, which is a repetition of one note. A well-known version of this song is " A little bit of bread and no cheese ".

Family *FRINGILLIDAE*.   Finches

CORN BUNTING   Length 7 in.
Emberiza calandra   Resident

This is the largest of the Buntings. It is not showy in appearance, but has its own charm for lovers of open country, where it may be met with perched on a railing or wire, singing its rattling song. In some places it is abundant.

HAUNT. Fairly general, especially in open country and on gorsy downs.

NEST. Of grass, moss and hair ; on the ground or in a low bush.

EGGS. 4 to 6, nearly white, with a reddish tinge, blotched and lined with dark brown. May, June.

FOOD. Mostly insects ; also seed.

NOTES. " Chip ". The bird perches on a telegraph wire to sing, or on the highest spray of a bush or hedge. The song is high and often begins with a few preliminary clucks before it breaks into a high tinkle like the shattering of glass or the jingling of a bunch of keys.

Family *FRINGILLIDAE*. Finches

SNOW BUNTING   Length 6½ in.
Plectrophenax nivalis   Chiefly winter visitor

    This Bunting is a winter visitor to the British Isles, not staying to breed except in the mountains of Scotland. It is a white bird, with black on the back, tail and wings. In winter this is somewhat obscured by brown striations on the back, head and breast. The female is browner. A twittering flock of these little white birds is a pretty but uncommon sight.

H A U N T. High moorlands and round the coast.

N E S T. Of grass, moss, roots, hair and feathers ; in a cranny in rocks or boulders.

E G G S. 5 to 8, bluish- or greenish-white, spotted and blotched with purplish- or dark-brown. May–July.

F O O D. Insects, chiefly flies, and weed-seeds.

N O T E S. The flight-note is a pretty, trilling twitter ; the song clear and sweet.

Family *FRINGILLIDAE*. Finches

REED BUNTING
Emberiza schoeniclus

Length 6 in.
Resident

The Reed Bunt-
ing sticks very
closely to its
own restricted
haunts, but may
be found in any
reed-bed. T h e
brown and white
plumage of the
male, with black
head and bib and
white collar, is
easily distin-
guished. T h i s
smart plumage
is slightly dulled
by brown tips
after the autumn
m o u l t. The
female is light
brown striated
w i t h chestnut

and dark brown, and has a heavy brown moustache
line.

HAUNT. Reed-beds and the reedy margins of
rivers, dykes and lakes.

NEST. Of grasses and hair ; among the reeds or
marsh grass.

EGGS. 3 to 6, browner in tone than the Yellowhammer's, and boldly blotched with nearly black.
April–July.

FOOD. Chiefly insects, and a little seed.

NOTES. Similar to those of other Buntings. The
song is a short and stuttering effort : about three repeti-
tions of a thin, metallic note, followed by a jumble of
squeaks.

Family *ORIOLIDAE*.   Orioles

GOLDEN ORIOLE
Oriolus oriolus

Length 9½ in.

Spring visitor

This handsome bird is a scarce migrant through south and east England, occasionally staying to nest. Male, brilliant yellow with black wings, black line from eye to red bill, and black tail with yellow corners. Female, yellowish-green, darker wings, pale beneath, slightly streaked. Usually hidden in trees.

NOTES.   Clear, fluty, challenging "Who are you-oo?"

Family *FRINGILLIDAE*.
Finches

ORTOLAN BUNTING
Emberiza hortulana

Length 6½ in.

Migrant

Seen migrating, chiefly at coast. Streaked brown above, rust beneath, green-grey breast and head, yellow throat, yellow eye-ring, coral bill and legs. Streaked immature lacks yellow and greenish; distinguished by eye-ring and bill.

LAPLAND BUNTING
Calcarius lapponicus

Length 6 in.

Migrant

Autumn, streaked plumage, white in tail; as Reed-Bunting. Distinguished by pale stripe on crown, black-streaked rump, mouse-like run, "ticky-tic", "teu" notes. Can show chestnut on nape and wing. Summer male, white-bordered black face and bib, chestnut nape.

HOUSE SPARROW
Passer domesticus

Length 5¾ in.
Resident

Of our small British birds, perhaps this is the most common and well-known, as it frequents the dwellings of man and even lives in the heart of great cities. The female is all brown, lacking the black bib and dark grey crown of the male.

HAUNT. Very general, especially on farms and near human habitations.

NEST. Of straw and feathers, loosely made in a hole in a building or wall, under eaves, in a Martin's nest, in creepers, and more rarely in a bush or tree, when the material is added to by roots and twigs.

EGGS. 5 or 6, grey or brown in general tone, completely covered with speckles and blotches. February–August.

FOOD. Grain, seed, insects.

NOTES. A variety of " chirps " and noisy " churrs ", usually a very loud and aggressive " chirp ".

TREE SPARROW
Passer montanus

Length 5½ in.

Resident

The Tree Sparrow differs from the House Sparrow in having a much smaller black bib and a bright brown cap. There is also a noticeable black patch on the white cheek, and the bird is slightly smaller and slimmer than the House Sparrow. The cock and hen birds are alike.

HAUNT. As its name implies, it is a bird of the country, and unlike the House Sparrow, avoids the dwellings of man.

NEST. Usually in a hole in a tree, quarry or old wall, in a colony with others. The materials are similar to those of the House Sparrow : an untidy collection of straw and feathers.

EGGS. 4 to 6, brownish, blotched and speckled all over. April–June.

FOOD. Insects and weed-seed.

NOTES. Similar to the House Sparrow's, but rather higher.

Family *BOMBYCILLIDAE*. Waxwings

WAXWING

Bombycilla garrulus

Length 7 in.

Winter visitor

This striking but uncommon winter visitor from northern Scandinavia reaches Britain during most winters, and is sometimes seen in considerable numbers in our eastern counties. The underparts are biscuit-colour, the back darker. A wide, tall crest sweeps back from the forehead, which is chestnut.

Under the tail is deep chestnut. The throat and a line above the eye are black; the wings are black, striped with white, and a long yellow line down the front edge extends to the tip. There is also a white and scarlet bar or patch on the wing. The red patch is composed of sealing-wax-like tips to the quills. The upper side of the tail, rump and lower back are grey, the tail shading to black with a buttercup-yellow tip.

FOOD. Mostly berries.

NOTES. Sometimes a thin trilling or wheezing note.

45

STARLING
Sturnus vulgaris

Length 8½ in.
Resident

Though nearly black, the Starling need never be confused with the Blackbird, owing to its short tail and straight flight. Also it waddles and runs about on the ground looking for food in a characteristic way, very unlike the long, springy hops of the Blackbird. The plumage is glossy with purple and green sheen. In winter it is speckled with white and buff tips. Immature birds are brownish.

HAUNT. Very general, even in the heart of London.

NEST. Of straw, grass and feathers ; in a hole, in masonry, under the eaves, or in a tree stack or creepers.

EGGS. 4 to 7, pale blue. April–June.

FOOD. Mostly insects and grubs which are harmful to agriculture, also fruit.

NOTES. The song is an exuberant medley of chatters, twitters and clicks, with occasional clear, high, long-drawn whistles. It also imitates other birds' notes and other familiar sounds.

Family *ALAUDIDAE*.   Larks

SKYLARK
Alauda arvensis

Length 7 in.
Resident

The Skylark is a very popular bird owing to its beautiful and joyful song as it hovers high in the blue. On the ground, the observer will notice that it does not hop, but walks or runs. The plumage is striated brown, with white on the outer tail feathers, which may be seen in flight. The brown crest is raised in excitement.

HAUNT.   Open country, fields and downs.

NEST.   Of dried grass ; on the ground.

EGGS.   3 to 5, densely covered with brown specks and freckles.   April–June.

FOOD.   Mostly insects and weed-seed ; also a small quantity of newly-sprouting shoots of grass, corn and other green.

NOTES.   A very beautiful exuberant song carried out on the wing, and too well known for further description.   There is also a liquid, trilling flight-note.

Family *ALAUDIDAE*. Larks

WOOD LARK

Length 6 in.

Lullula arborea

Resident

This brown, striated bird may be distinguished from the Skylark by its smaller size and by the much shorter tail, which is noticeable, both on the ground and in flight when the bird hovers overhead. There is also a small blackish and white mark on the edge of the folded wing and a more distinct crest on the head. The most noticeable difference of all is the song, which has an extraordinary power of fascination.

HAUNT. Tree-clad and open country.

NEST. Of dried grass ; on the ground.

EGGS. 3 or 4, speckled all over with bright brown (not so densely as those of the Skylark). March–May.

FOOD. Insects and seed.

NOTES. A clear triple call-note, also a beautiful but rather wistful song, quite unlike the Skylark's. This song is rather simple, only consisting of a few notes descending in a silvery minor key, often difficult to locate.

Family *ALAUDIDAE*.   Larks

SHORE LARK
Eremophila alpestris

Length 6½ in.
Winter visitor

The Shore Lark is an uncommon winter visitor, chiefly to the east and south-east coasts of England. The plumage is primrose-yellow on the throat, and primrose and black on the head. The upper part of the breast is black, the underparts nearly white, and the back and wings brown. In late autumn, when the bird is usually seen, the black on the head is mottled with yellow. The female has no long crest feathers on the head and not so much black.

HAUNT.   Usually the shore, or nearby.

FOOD.   Insects, small shellfish, and crustaceans picked up on the shore, and seeds from seaside fields.

NOTES.   " Peep " or " chee-eep ".   It does not sing while with us.

PIED WAGTAIL

Length 7 in.

Motacilla alba yarrellii

Resident

This slender, dainty little black and white bird is easily distinguished. On the ground it runs very fast in short rushes, wagging its tail up and down at each pause. The female is grey on the back and has a little less black on the breast. In winter the back of the male is dark grey and both birds have only a crescent of black on the breast. Also known as " Water Wagtail " and " Dishwasher ". It is the British subspecies of the Continental White Wagtail.

HAUNT.   General, not necessarily near water.

NEST.   Of dried grass, roots, hair and wool; in a hole, usually in a bank or wall.

EGGS.   4 to 6, whitish, covered all over with grey speckles.   April–June.

FOOD.   Insects, chiefly flies.   A most useful bird in keeping down flies and small insect pests.

NOTES.   A liquid " tu-reep " or " tschis-seek "; also a low song composed of similar notes.

Family *MOTACILLIDAE.* Wagtails and Pipits

GREY WAGTAIL

Motacilla cinerea

Length 7 in.

Resident

The sulphur-yellow breast of this lovely, slender little bird at once distinguishes it f r o m the Pied Wagtail. Also, it may be distinguished from the Yellow Wagtail by its slate-blue b a c k. In the winter the black throat is replaced by white. The female is paler grey above, and lacks the black throat.

HAUNT. Rocky streamlets, rivers, ponds and woodland brooks.

N E S T. Of rootlets, grass and hair ; in a hole in a river-bank, wall or rock.

E G G S. 4 to 6, very like those of the Pied Wagtail, but sometimes browner. April–June.

F O O D. Insects, chiefly flies.

N O T E S. The flight-note is sharper than that of the Pied, and more silvery in tone : " te-seep ". The song is clear and musical, sometimes trilling.

Family *MOTACILLIDAE*.   Wagtails and Pipits

WHITE WAGTAIL
Motacilla alba alba

Length 7 in.

Migrant

The White Wagtail, the Continental subspecies of the British Pied Wagtail, is a bird of passage and uncommon summer visitor, differing from the Pied in having a grey back.   It is usually seen here in spring and summer, when the back of the male Pied is black.   The chin, throat and nape are black, as with the Pied.   The Pied and White females, immatures and autumn migrants are less easy to distinguish, though the female White has little or no black on the crown.

HAUNT.   Lakes, streams, coasts, sewage farms.

NEST.   Of moss, grass and wool ; in a hole in a wall or bank.

EGGS.   4 to 7, white or bluish-white, thickly freckled with grey or grey-brown.   May.

FOOD.   Flies and other small insects.

NOTES.   Both flight-note and song are strikingly like those of the Pied Wagtail.

Family *MOTACILLIDAE*.   Wagtails and Pipits

BLUE-HEADED WAGTAIL   Length 6½ in.

Motacilla flava flava Spring and Summer visitor

The Blue-headed Wagtail, the Continental subspecies of the British Yellow Wagtail, is an uncommon bird of passage not always easy to distinguish from the Yellow Wagtail. The plumage is the same, except for the head, which, instead of being yellow and olive, is slate-blue with a bold white stripe above the eye. A white line divides the bright yellow underparts from the slaty cheek. The back is olive-green, the wings brownish, barred with nearly white. The female is very like that of the Yellow Wagtail and is even harder to distinguish.

The notes, habits, nest and eggs are all like those of the Yellow Wagtail, as is the food, which consists of flies and other small insects.   It occasionally stays to breed in the British Isles.

53

Family *MOTACILLIDAE*.   Wagtails and Pipits

YELLOW WAGTAIL   Length 6½ in.
Motacilla flava flavissima   April–September

This is one of the smaller Wagtails, and is most
dainty and lovely in colour.   It is the British subspecies
of the Continental Blue-headed Wagtail.   It is a
summer visitor or bird of passage, chiefly in pasture
land.   The plumage is bright sulphur-yellow beneath,
and olive above, with blackish tail and wings and
white outer tail feathers.   The female is rather browner
above and paler beneath.

HAUNT.   Pastures, fields and marshes.

NEST.   Of grass, rootlets, moss, hair, wool and
feathers; on the ground or in a bank.

EGGS.   4 to 6, whitish, freckled with grey or brown.
April–June.

FOOD.   Flies and other small insects.

NOTES.   The usual note is a sharp high " tseep ";
the song a liquid, warbling, chirruping snatch.

Family *MOTACILLIDAE*. Wagtails and Pipits

MEADOW PIPIT or TITLARK Length 5¾ in.
Anthus pratensis   Resident

This is a rather slim and dainty little brown and buff, striated bird, with the Wagtail family's distinctive and nimble run and walk. It does not hop.

H A U N T. Downs, moors and fields.

N E S T. Of dried grass, lined with hair or wool ; on the ground, well hidden in grass or heather.

E G G S. 4 to 6, densely covered with grey-brown or chocolate speckles. April–June.

F O O D. Mostly insects and a small quantity of weed-seed.

N O T E S. The noticeable alarm cry is " peep peep peep " ; there is also a quiet little note " tit " or " pipit " when walking daintily through the grass. Song : a repetition of " peep peep " as it mounts into the air, growing faster till it planes down again, wings stiffly spread and tail tilted up, with a clicking, whirring twitter, " pe-pe-pe-pe-pe-pe ".

Family *MOTACILLIDAE*.   Wagtails and Pipits

TREE PIPIT
Anthus trivialis

Length 6 in.

April–September

The Tree Pipit is very similar to the Meadow Pipit in appearance, chiefly d i f f e r i n g in its h a b i t a t.   T h e p l u m a g e is buff beneath and light brown above, much striated all over. It is a s u m m e r visitor.

H A U N T.   Fairly open, tree - clad country, and the outskirts of woods.

N E S T.   Like the Meadow Pipit's, of g r a s s ; o n t h e ground, concealed in long grass or other herbage.

E G G S. 4 to 6, very varying, more distinctly blotched than those of the last species. May, June.

F O O D.   Mostly insects and a little weed-seed.

N O T E S.   Similar to the Meadow Pipit's, but instead of rising and descending to the ground in song, it takes off from a branch and planes down to it again.   The song is more musical and has a sweet rallentando at the end : " tweedle, tweedle, sweet, sweet, sweet ".

Family *MOTACILLIDAE*.   Wagtails and Pipits

ROCK PIPIT
Anthus spinoletta

Length 6½ in.

Resident

This is a dainty, striated bird, differing in appearance from the Meadow Pipit in its larger size and the greyer tone of its plumage, and also in its habitat.

HAUNT. The rocky coast. It keeps most strictly to the rocks and cliffs, except in winter, when it may be driven to mudflats and estuaries for food.

NEST. Of grass and hair, and sometimes seaweed ; in a cliff-hole or crevice, or behind a clump of thrift.

EGGS. 4 or 5, similar to other Pipits', very densely speckled with grey or grey-brown. May and June.

FOOD. Insects, chiefly flies, and a few small marine creatures.

NOTES. The alarm- or flight-note is a loud " peep peep ". The song is like that of other Pipits. It mounts into the air uttering " peep-peep-peep-peep ", and planes down sharply with a metallic clicking " pe-pe-pe-pe-pe ", which grows faster and faster till it dies away as the bird alights.

NUTHATCH
Sitta europaea

Length 5½ in.
Resident

The Nuthatch is a pretty and interesting trunk-creeping bird, walking up or down the tree-trunk with equal ease. The plumage of the upper parts is soft slate-blue, and beneath it is buff, shading to chestnut-red on the flanks.

HAUNT. Woods, parks and trees in gardens.

NEST. Of dead leaves, grass and bark ; in a hole, usually in a tree-trunk. The entrance is filled up with mud, leaving only a round hole just sufficient for the bird to pass through. I remember hearing of an enterprising bird which stole some cement and made a really good job of it !

EGGS. 5 to 8, not unlike the Tree-Creeper's, though larger : white spotted with light red. April–June.

FOOD. Mostly insects, also nuts, berries and seeds.

NOTES. A clear whistle, " toy toy ", and other ringing notes, and a metallic trill.

Family *CERTHIIDAE*.   Creepers

TREE CREEPER
Length 5 in.

Certhia familiaris
Resident

This quiet, mouse-like little bird may be seen making its way up the trunk of a tree as easily as a fly crawls up a wall. It seems to find a dainty morsel in every crack in the bark. Its movements are jerky, but it is very inconspicuous against the trunk. The plumage is striated-brown above and white beneath.

HAUNT.   Woods, parks and trees in gardens.

NEST.   Of twigs, grass, moss, bark, hair and feathers ; in a crevice in a tree, behind loose bark or the stem of a creeper.

EGGS.   5 to 9, white, spotted with red-brown at the large end. May, June.

FOOD.   Insects and larvae.

NOTES.   It has a high note, " treep ", uttered when feeding or in flight, and a short song " tee, tee, tee, sissi-tee ".

Family *REGULIDAE*.   Goldcrests or Kinglets

FIRECREST
Length 3½ in.

Regulus ignicapillus
Winter visitor

An uncommon winter visitor, chiefly to south England.   It is like the Goldcrest in appearance, but greener above and whiter beneath with a shade of gold on the sides of the neck and a brighter crest.   The clearest distinction is the black stripe through the eye and the white one above and below it.   Haunt, food and notes similar to Goldcrest's.

GOLDCREST

Regulus regulus

Length 3½ in.

Resident

The tiny Goldcrest, commonly called Golden-crested Wren, is the smallest European bird. Though inconspicuous in its favourite haunts among fir branches, it is a gem among birds, with its soft olive plumage, bright crest and fine dark bill and legs. The female's crest is yellow, lacking the fiery touch of the male's.

HAUNT. Usually woods, copses and larch or fir-plantations.

NEST. Of moss, lichens and spiders' web, cleverly woven together into a tiny, basket-like nest, lined with feathers and hanging under the branch of a fir tree.

EGGS. 7 to 10, very small, white, covered with very tiny, faint red-brown specks. April–June.

FOOD. Insects, including greenfly and many of minute size.

NOTES. There is a very tiny, high, trilling song like the tinkling of a fairy bell, often difficult to locate. Call-notes " si si si ".

CRESTED TIT
Parus cristatus

Length 4½ in.
Resident

This small, chubby Tit, brownish above and pale beneath, with its sibilant, purring call-note, is resident in a comparatively small area of Scotland, chiefly centred around the beautiful Spey Valley. The crest is white dappled with black; the cheeks white outlined by a black band leading round to the narrow black collar and bib.

HAUNT. Pine and mixed forests.

NEST. Of moss, hair and occasionally feathers in a hole, usually in a rotting tree stump.

EGGS. Usually 5 or 6, white, zoned with chestnut blotches.

FOOD. Chiefly insects and larvae, also pine-seeds and berries.

NOTES. There is a high " si-si-si " like that of other tits, but the only really distinctive note is a low, purring trill.

BEARDED TIT or REEDLING   Length 6½ in.
Panurus biarmicus   Resident

If you are lucky enough to see this rare Reedling, you will easily recognise it by its wedge-shaped tail, and light-red and pale-grey plumage. The male has a light blue-grey head and very conspicuous black moustache lines, wide at the top and terminating in points at the base of the neck on either side. The wings are widely striped with rufous and grey and the back is tawny. The female is not so bright, and lacks the grey head and black moustache.

HAUNT.   Reed-beds, only in East Anglia.

NEST.   Of sedges, lined with fine grass and reed-flowers ; just above the water, in herbage.

EGGS.   5 to 7, whitish, speckled and lined with brown.   April–August.

FOOD.   Mostly insects and small freshwater molluscs.

NOTES.   " Cht, cht ", and a twanging " ping ".

Family *PARIDAE*.   Titmice

GREAT TIT   Length 5½ in.
Parus major   Resident

All the Tit family are acrobats and interesting to watch as they hang upside down on the twigs in search of insects, or come to our windows in winter and cling to a coconut or bone hung up for them. The Great Tit is the largest of the tribe, and is a handsome bird with yellow, green and blue plumage, a black and white head, and a black band beneath from chin to tail.

HAUNT. General.

NEST. Of grass, moss, hair and feathers ; in a hole in a tree or wall, or in a pump, flowerpot or even letter-box.

EGGS. 6 or 7, occasionally 12 or more, white, spotted with light red. April or May.

FOOD. Insects, nuts, seeds ; also fat and scraps.

NOTES. " Si si si " and a sharp " chink ". The song, " tea-cher ", is a high and a low metallic note repeated several times.

COAL TIT
Parus ater

Length 4¼ in.

Resident

The Coal Tit is easily distinguished from the Great and Blue Tits by its more sombre colouring. The upper parts are olive-brown and the underparts buff, palest on the breast. The cap and throat are black, the cheeks white. The white nape is the easiest characteristic by which to distinguish it from the Marsh Tit.

HAUNT. Gardens and wooded country.

NEST. Of moss, grass and hair or wool; in a hole, low down in a wall or stump, or even in the ground.

EGGS. 6 to 11, white, spotted with light red; like the Blue Tit's. April or May.

FOOD. Mostly insects; also beech-mast and seeds.

NOTES. Rather similar to those of other Tits. The short song has been described as " If-hee, if-hee, if-hee ".

Family *PARIDAE*. Titmice

MARSH TIT
Parus palustris

Length 4½ in.
Resident

The Marsh Tit is another brownish Tit, distinguishable from the Coal Tit by the lighter underparts, black cap lacking the Coal Tit's white nape patch, and by having a much smaller extent of black on the throat. It also lacks the bar on the wing.

H A U N T. Gardens, woods and marshes.

N E S T. Of moss, wool, hair and rabbit-fur ; in a hole in a tree, or occasionally in the ground.

E G G S. 5 to 9, white, speckled with light red. April–June.

F O O D. Insects and small seeds.

NOTES. A loud " pitchoo ", a harsh, low, nasal, repeated " char ", a high " si-si-si ", and others. The song is a repetition of two or three notes.

WILLOW TIT
Parus montanus

Length 4½ in.
Resident

Almost exactly like the Marsh Tit; but the cap instead of being glossy black is dull sooty and extends further down the nape, and there is a pale stripe on the secondaries formed by light feather-edges. The black bib tends to be more extensive, the flanks more buff. It is less common and more local than the Marsh Tit.

BLUE TIT

Parus caeruleus

Length 4½ in.

Resident

The Blue or Tom-Tit is another very popular little acrobat, smaller than the Great Tit, and even more often seen hanging upside down on a twig or coconut. The plumage is primrose-yellow on the underparts and a greyish-blue and green above. The head is blue and white.

HAUNT. Very general.

NEST. Of moss, wool and feathers ; in a hole in a tree or wall, or in an odd place such as a pump, letter-box or street-lamp.

EGGS. 7 or 8 or more, white, spotted with light red ; like those of the Great Tit, but smaller. April or May.

FOOD. Chiefly insects. It is most useful in destroying greenfly and other aphids and many insect pests. It also eats nuts, fat and scraps if these are hung up for it.

NOTES. " Tsee, tsee, ch-ch-ch-ch-ch ", " si-si-si " and others. Song, two or three high notes and a trill.

LONG-TAILED TIT
Aegithalos caudatus

Length 5½ in.

Resident

This tiny acrobat is mostly tail, and without the extra length of this is a very tiny Tit. Its call-notes and antics are like those of other Tits, as it works through the trees or bushes in search of insects, usually in a party of about half a dozen. The plumage is white and black, tinged with red. The illustration shows also the white-headed Northern race.

HAUNT. Hedgerows, copses and woods.

NEST. Of moss, lichens, wool and spiders' webs, well felted together and lined with countless feathers ; in a bush or hedge. The nest is very deep and domed, the entrance hole being at the side near the top. In this stifling, feathery ball are squeezed, at night, about twelve chicks and both parents.

EGGS. 6 to 15, white, speckled with light red. April or May.

FOOD. Mostly insects.

NOTES. Usually a low " zup " continuously repeated.

Family *SYLVIIDAE*. Warblers

WOOD WARBLER
Phylloscopus sibilatrix

Length 5 in.

End April–August

This dainty summer visitor differs from the Willow Warbler and Chiffchaff in its greater size and rather lighter greenish-olive upper plumage. The underparts are white, the throat and the sides of the neck are yellow, with a very noticeable yellow streak above the eye. It is less common than the three Warblers which follow.

HAUNT. Among trees, especially beeches and oaks.

NEST. A domed nest of grass, moss, leaves and hair is made on the ground.

EGGS. 5 or 6, white, speckled with dark purplish-or brownish-red. May.

FOOD. Insects, chiefly small ones.

NOTES. Rather similar to those of the Willow Warbler : " tee-oo ". The song is a sibilant stutter, breaking into a shivering, silvery trill, punctuated now and again with a low insistent note repeated several times.

CHIFFCHAFF
Phylloscopus collybita

Length 4¼ in.
March–October

This small War-
bler is a summer
visitor, very like
the Willow War-
bler in habits and
almost identical
in appearance.
The best distinc-
tion between the
two is the song,
and as the Chiff-
chaff utters his al-
most incessantly
it is a good guide.
The plumage is
olive in tone, buf-
fish-white be-
neath. The legs
are darker than those of the Willow Warbler.

HAUNT. General, except in Scotland, especially among trees.

NEST. Domed like that of the Willow
Warbler; varying from a few inches to a few
feet from the ground, in herbage or bushes.

EGGS. 5 to 7, white spotted with brown. May.

FOOD. Insects.

NOTES. The song, from which it gets its
name, is a familiar sound in spring; an endlessly
repeated " chiff-chaff " or " chiff-chiff "; sometimes punctuated by a low " chirrick ". Call-
note like Willow Warbler's.

Family *SYLVIIDAE*. Warblers

WILLOW WARBLER

Phylloscopus trochilus

Length 4¼ in.

April–September

A small, quiet but abundant visitor to all bushes and trees in spring and summer. The plumage is olive a b o v e and buffish - w h i t e beneath, the legs usually light-brown.

HAUNT. Very general, especially in woods and copses.

NEST. Chiefly of grass, lined w i t h feathers, and domed; on the ground in herbage or grass.

EGGS. 6 to 8, white, spotted with light red. May.

FOOD. Insects ; including small flies, blight and numerous other kinds, both large and minute.

NOTES. The call-note is a plaintive " too-eet ", similar, though softer in tone, to that of the Chaffinch. The song is a very sweet descending cadence, not loud but clear and carrying to a distance. It is one of the most familiar sounds of spring.

Family *SYLVIIDAE*. Warblers

SEDGE WARBLER — Length 5 in.

End April–September

Acrocephalus schoenobaenus

This small summer visitor is one of the more common Warblers, distinct both in appearance and song. The warm brown of the upper plumage is streaked with lighter colour and with almost black on the head and back, and there is a noticeable light line over the eye.

HAUNT. Marshes, ponds, ditches and rivers.

NEST. Of grass, moss, stalks and hair ; in herbage, low bushes or long grass.

EGGS. 5 or 6, greenish-yellow, mottled all over with brown. May.

FOOD. Chiefly aquatic insects and their larvae.

NOTES. There are various notes, including a scolding " churr " and an excited " tek, tek ". The song is a loud and varied chatter, usually noticed coming from the ditch or herbage in which the bird is hidden. This twitter contains surprisingly deep notes, followed by harsh chatters and squeaks and bubbling warbles.

Family *SYLVIIDAE*. Warblers

REED WARBLER
Length 5 in.

Acrocephalus scirpaceus   End April–September

This summer visitor is inconspicuous in its brown plumage, lighter beneath. It has not the distinctive markings of the Sedge Warbler.

HAUNT. Reed-beds, marshes, etc., in southern England, spreading as far north as Yorkshire and rare in W. Wales and Cornwall.

NEST. A beautifully constructed deep cup, made chiefly of grass, moss and wool, and suspended between reed stems. Occasionally a drier situation is chosen in a bush.

EGGS. 4 or 5, greenish-white, blotched with olive. May–July.

FOOD. Insects.

NOTES. The song is a warble containing some of the harsh notes of the Sedge Warbler, but lacking the variety and exuberance of that bird. There is also a scolding " churr ".

Family *SYLVIIDAE.* Warblers

MARSH WARBLER

Length 5 in.

Acrocephalus palustris

End May–August

A summer visitor very like the Reed Warbler in appearance, but less common. Very local in parts of S. England. The olive-brown plumage of the upper parts is slightly paler and less warm in tone. The underparts are buff, shading to nearly white.

HAUNT. Reed-beds, osiers, and thick vegetation and thickets.

NEST. Of grass, moss and hair; suspended between the stems of herbage.

EGGS. 4 or 5, nearly white, blotched with purplish-grey or brown. June or July.

FOOD. Insects.

NOTES. Similar to those of the last species. The song is sweeter and more variable, including the notes of other birds. Like many other Warblers, it sings at night as well as by day.

BLACKCAP

Length 5½ in.

Sylvia atricapilla

April–October

This Warbler is a summer visitor, though, like the Chiffchaff, it has been known to winter in south-west England. The male may be easily distinguished by its grey-brown plumage and black cap; and the red-brown cap of the female is almost equally noticeable.

HAUNT.   Chiefly wooded places and gardens.

NEST.   Of dried grass, fibrous rootlets and hair; in brambles, creepers or a bush.

EGGS.   4 or 5, yellowish-white, mottled with reddish-brown.   May.

FOOD.   Insects, including flies and larvae; also berries.

NOTES.   The scolding " churr " and " tak-tak-tak ", as well as the song, can be confused with those of the Garden Warbler, but the song is louder, higher and shorter.   It is a clear, strong, melodious warble.

Family *SYLVIIDAE*. Warblers

WHITETHROAT

Sylvia communis

Length 5½ in.

April–October

This Warbler is a summer visitor and may be distinguished from others by its conspicuous white throat, especially when this is swelling in song and the grey feathers of the crown are raised in excitement. The sexes are similar, but the female has a less pink tone on the breast and lacks the grey head of the male in summer plumage. Both are rusty-tinted above and have white outer tail-feathers.

HAUNT. Copses and hedgerows, etc.

NEST. Of dried grass, rootlets and hair; in a bush, brambles or herbage near the ground.

EGGS. 4 to 6, nearly white, speckled with greyish- or reddish-brown. May or June.

FOOD. Mostly insects; also berries.

NOTES. A scolding, ticking note and low " dzer " or " charr ". The song is a short, harsh warble, often sung excitedly as the bird flutters up from a hedge and drops back into it again like an arrow.

LESSER WHITETHROAT

Length 5¼ in.

Sylvia curruca

April–September

This is another summer visitor, chiefly to south England, excluding Cornwall and west Wales. It is secretive and less abundant than the last. The plumage is grey-brown above and whitish beneath, with a grey head, dark cheeks and white on outer tail-feathers.

HAUNT. Hedges, woods and copses.

NEST. Of fine dry grass and rootlets; in a bush or hedge.

EGGS. 4 to 6, nearly white, spotted with brown and pale grey.　May or June.

FOOD. Mostly insects, including blight; also berries.

NOTES. Various, including an excited " tak ". The song is a very loud rattling trill, usually preceded by a soft, low warble.　This rattle is usually heard from a hidden perch in a tree.

Family *SYLVIIDAE*.   Warblers

GRASSHOPPER WARBLER   Length 5 in.

Locustella naevia   End April–September

This Warbler is an extremely secretive summer visitor with olive-brown plumage, mottled and streaked chiefly on the upper parts. It usually remains hidden in thick herbage or low scrub where it creeps about in search of insects, and is not detected except by its strange, soft, reeling song.

HAUNT. Downs, commons and marshes.

NEST. Of dried grass and moss ; in a tuft of long grass or reeds, or in a low bush or heather.

EGGS. 4 to 6, nearly white, finely speckled with light red. May–July.

FOOD. Insects.

NOTES. The most distinctive thing about this little bird is its whirring song, which is sometimes as continuous as the sound of a grasshopper, though unlike it in tone. It is a strange purring sound, rising and falling in volume. There is also a short note " tic ".

GARDEN WARBLER
Sylvia borin

Length 5½ in.
End April–September

The Garden Warbler is a secretive but quite common summer visitor. The plumage is not conspicuous. It is brown of a rather olive or grey shade above and very pale b u f f beneath.

HAUNT. Chiefly woods and copses and thick covert.

NEST. Fraily built of dried grass and hair; in brambles or a bush.

EGGS. 4 or 5, yellowish-white, mottled with reddish- or greyish-brown. May.

FOOD. Mostly insects, including greenfly and other small flies ; and sometimes fruit.

NOTES. Rather like those of the White-throats. The song is a very beautiful low warble, longer and sweeter than that of the Blackcap.

DARTFORD WARBLER

Sylvia undata

Length 5 in.

Resident

This uncommon little Warbler is the only resident bird of its family. It is found only in a few southern counties. The plumage of the male is dark grey-brown above and purple-red-Devon-soil beneath. In winter there are whitish striations on the throat. The female is not quite so dark a grey above and has a browner tone; the underparts are lighter. The general appearance of both is of a very small bird with a rather long tail.

HAUNT. Gorse bushes and copses.

NEST. Of dried grass, gorse and rootlets, lined with hair or wool; in a gorse bush or heather.

EGGS. 4 to 6, nearly white, mottled with light grey and brown. April–July.

FOOD. Chiefly insects, both large and small; also a few berries in winter.

NOTES. A clear triple call-note; also a scolding note similar to the Whitethroat's. Song, a rippling warble.

MISTLE THRUSH

Turdus viscivorus

Length 10½ in.

Resident

A large thrush differing from the more abundant Song Thrush in its greater size and greyer-toned plumage. The upper parts are grey-brown, and the breast nearly white, s p o t t e d with dark brown.

H A U N T. General, i n c l u d i n g fields, woods, gardens and copses.

N E S T.   O f grass, roots, moss and mud, lined with dry grass ; usually in the fork of a tree, if there is one available ; otherwise a bush or wall may be selected.

E G G S.   4 or 5, whitish, spotted with reddish- and greyish-brown.   February–May.

F O O D.   Snails, slugs, worms, grubs, insects and berries.

N O T E S.   A harsh " churr " and a sharp " chick ".   The song is loud, but lacks the fullness and variety of that of the Song Thrush.   It is a short phrase constantly repeated.   The bird is also known as the " Storm-Cock ", from the way it will perch on a tree and sing into the teeth of a gale.

SONG THRUSH
Turdus philomelos

Length 9 in.

Resident

This well-known and well-loved bird is one of our best songsters, and is familiar to us everywhere, especially in gardens, where it hops upon the lawn and pulls at a resisting worm. The plumage is brown above and buffish-white beneath, with very dark brown spots on the breast.

HAUNT. General.

NEST. Of twigs, grass and moss, with a smooth lining of mud; in a bush, hedge, tree or creeper.

EGGS. 4 or 5, of a beautiful bright turquoise-blue, spotted with black. February–July.

FOOD. Worms, slugs, snails, grubs and insects; also berries. The bird smashes the snail-shells on a stone.

NOTES. A rather quiet " chick " and scolding " chook-chook ". The song is loud, clear and full. It sometimes resembles " did he do it, did he do it, Judy did " and " Come out, come out ".

BLACKBIRD   Length 10 in.

Turdus merula   Resident

The Blackbird is one of our most familiar birds, especially in the garden, and as a songster it is second to none, some people preferring its rich, full whistle to the warbles and deep ejaculations of the Nightingale. The plumage of the cock is black, with a crocus-yellow bill.   The female and immature birds are dark brown, darkest on the tail and wings, with dark brown bills. Patches of white are not uncommon on blackbirds, and complete albinos also occur.

HAUNT.   General.

NEST.   Of grass, rootlets and mud, lined with finer grass ; in a bush, creeper or tree.

EGGS.   4 to 6, greenish-blue, finely speckled with warm brown.   March–July.

FOOD.   Worms, snails, grubs, insects and fruit.

NOTES.   The loud clattering cry of a startled Blackbird is familiar.   It rises with a chattering yell and subsides again with a few protesting clucks.   Another alarm-note is a loud, persistent " pink, pink ".   At dusk it sometimes utters this note continuously, and apparently aimlessly.   The song is a rich, sweet whistle.

FIELDFARE
Turdus pilaris

Length 10 in.
Winter visitor

The Fieldfare is only a winter visitor, but in the colder months it may be seen, sometimes with other members of the Thrush family, in the fields or searching the hedges for haws and other berries. In size it comes between the Song- and Mistle-Thrushes, but the grey head and rump are distinctive. The back is chestnut-brown, and the lighter breast is covered with nearly black markings. The wings and tail are very dark brown.

HAUNT. Chiefly in fields and open country.
FOOD. Worms, grubs, insects and berries.
NOTES. A harsh " chack ". As in the case of the Redwing, the song is not often heard in this country. An attempt to warble may be made in early spring before the birds leave, but the full song is reserved for the nesting season.

Family *TURDIDAE*.   Thrushes

REDWING   Length 8¼ in.

Turdus musicus   Winter visitor

This beautiful Thrush is a winter visitor. In size and general appearance it resembles the Song-Thrush, but there is a warm, pinkish-chestnut area on the flanks and a noticeable light stripe over the eye ; and the whole tone of the plumage is deeper and richer than that of the Song-Thrush. The spots on the breast are elongated, forming striations.

H A U N T.   Chiefly in open country.

F O O D.   Chiefly worms, grubs and insects ; also berries.

N O T E S.   A soft " took ", also a churring cry, and in flight a thin squeak, " seeep ".   A low, warbling sub-song is heard in winter.   The full song, which is occasionally heard before the birds leave in spring, is a short, clear snatch.

RING OUZEL

Turdus torquatus

Length 9½ in.

April–October

This is a summer visitor, in appearance not unlike a Blackbird with a white crescent on the breast. T h e female's plumage is slightly dappled by whitish edgings to the feathers. She is lighter, a n d t h e white gorget is tinged with brown.

HAUNT. Wild tors, hills, moors and mountains.

NEST. Of dry grass beneath a tuft of heather or grass, or in the cleft of a crag.

EGGS. 4 or 5, blue-green blotched with rufous. May.

FOOD. Insects, grubs, snails, slugs and berries.

NOTES. A scolding " chack-chack-chack " and a high whistle. Often the Ring Ouzel is silent as it skims over a boulder and disappears like a black shadow. The song is short and clear, often only repeating 3 or 4 notes.

ROBIN

Length 5½ in.

Erithacus rubecula

Resident

The Robin, or Redbreast, is perhaps the best-known and best-loved of all our birds, owing to its friendly and intelligent ways and bright plumage. The cock and hen are alike (contrary to tradition !). The young are brown and speckled.

HAUNT. Very general.

NEST. Of grass, wool, moss and hair ; in a hole in a wall, tree or bank, or any other convenient niche. Very often it is in an old kettle or pail, or even indoors on a bookshelf, or in a church.

EGGS. 5 or 6, white, speckled with light red. February–July.

FOOD. Chiefly insects of all kinds, and worms ; also crumbs and other scraps ; sometimes fruit or berries.

NOTES. A sharp " tic, tic ", and a faint, high, long-drawn wheeze. The song is clear, high and very varied, consisting of many sweet notes and twitters.

REDSTART

Length 5½ in.

Phoenicurus phoenicurus

April–October

The Redstart is a summer visitor, chiefly to hill and dale and woodland, rather similar in size and general characteristics to the Robin, but far more retiring and uncommon. The plumage of the male is grey on the upper parts, with a bright chestnut-red rump and tail. The breast and flanks are also chestnut. The cheeks and throat are black, the forehead white. The female is paler and more brown in tone, lacking the black throat and rufous breast, but she has also the characteristic light red tail.

HAUNT. Not very definite, usually near trees.

NEST. Of dry grass, rootlets, moss, hair and feathers ; in a hole in a tree, wall or quarry.

EGGS. 5 or 6, pale turquoise-blue. May, June.

FOOD. Insects.

NOTES. A Chat-like " wee-chit " and a plaintive " weet ". The song is short, rather like the Robin's, but less varied.

BLACK REDSTART
Phoenicurus ochrurus

Length 5½ in.

Chiefly migrant

The Black Redstart differs from the last species in being grey and black all over except for the orange-rufous rump and tail. The cheeks, throat and breast are nearly black, the upper parts grey. The female is much lighter and more grey-brown in tone, differing from the female common Redstart in being greyer. She also has the chestnut tail.

HAUNT. Buildings, ruins, rocks, rubble, rubbish-dumps. On migration, chiefly south, east and west coasts, and a few winter in the south-west, while in south-east coastal towns and in the bombed areas in London it has bred in some numbers.

NEST. Of grass, moss, hair and sometimes feathers, in a hole or ledge in ruins, or a roof, or in a cleft in a rock.

EGGS. 4 to 6, usually white, April or May.

FOOD. Chiefly insects.

NOTES. A short " tic ". It also has a simple, high-pitched song.

WHINCHAT
Length 5 in.

Saxicola rubetra
April–September

The Whinchat differs from the Stonechat in being a summer visitor, and in lacking the black head and white collar of the male Stonechat, but both are typical Chats in their characteristics. The male has a black cheek and white line above the eye, a white bar on the wing, and white at the base of the tail on each side.   The breast is pinkish buff, shading to nearly white, and the back is brown and much striated.   The female lacks the black and white on the face.

HAUNT. The haunts are like those of the Stonechat, but it is even more a bird of open moorland.

NEST. Of grass, moss and hair ; on or near the ground.

EGGS.   4 to 6, greenish-blue, sometimes faintly speckled with rufous.   May and June.

FOOD.   Insects of all kinds.

NOTES.   The song is short and squeaky.   The usual notes, while twitching the tail, are " tu ", " tic-tic-tic ".

STONECHAT

Length 5 in.

Saxicola torquata

Resident

A smart and dainty little bird with a distinctive note and a distinctive way of jerking and flirting its wings and tail, especially on alighting.   The plumage of the male is chestnut-pink beneath and dark brown above, with a white bar on the wing and a whitish patch on the rump.   The head is black, with a showy white collar.   The female lacks the black head and white collar.

HAUNT.   Chiefly commons and open, gorse-clad country, especially near the coast.

NEST.   Of grass, moss, hair and wool ; well hidden in a low gorse bush or similar position.

EGGS.   4 to 6, blue-green, very finely speckled with red-brown.   April or May.

FOOD.   Chiefly insects and grubs.   It has been recorded as very useful in keeping down insects and maggots which attack sheep, as well as many other pests.

NOTES.   A pebble-clicking alarm-note constantly repeated, " wee-chat, wee-chat-chat ", the first note being high and sharp.   The song is short and cheerful, sometimes uttered in short, dancing song-flight.

Family *TURDIDAE*. Thrushes

WHEATEAR
Oenanthe oenanthe

Length 5¾ in.
March–October

The Wheatear is a most attractive summer visitor of moorlands and hillsides, readily distinguished by the flash of its conspicuous white rump, as it flits along near the ground. The plumage is pale g r e y above and cream - colour beneath, with a warmer tinge on the breast. The earcoverts, wings and the tip of the tail are nearly black. The female is more brown in tone, but also has the noticeable white rump.

HAUNT. Downs, moors, hills, cliffs and open places.

NEST. In an old rabbit-hole, under a boulder or clod or in a hole in a stone wall.

EGGS. 4 to 6, pale turquoise-blue. April or May.

FOOD. Chiefly insects and small snails and grubs. It is invaluable in destroying pests.

NOTES. The song and notes are similar to those of other Chats, though the former is less restricted and short.

GREENLAND WHEATEAR, *Oenanthe oenanthe leucorrhoa*, 6¼ in. long, has a reddish tinge on the breast, a browner grey back, and an upright stance. It is only an uncommon migrant (subspecies of the above) not easy to distinguish.

NIGHTINGALE

Luscinia megarhynchos

Length 6½ in.

April–September

This bird, famous for its song, is a rather shy, retiring summer visitor. The plumage is smooth brown with paler underparts and chestnut tail. The cock and hen are alike.

HAUNT. Woods and thickets.

NEST. Chiefly of dead leaves and grass; on or near the ground at the base of a bush.

EGGS, 4 to 6, olive-blue or olive-brown. May.

FOOD. Chiefly insects, g r u b s a n d worms; also berries.

NOTES. The call-note is a plaintive " hweet ", like Chaffinch or Willow-Warbler. Alarm, a low, grating " chrr ". The song is often loud and contains very deep, full notes, as well as low trills and warbles. It sings as much in the day-time as at night; in fact, from my own experience, I should say more; but the song is naturally more noticed at night.

RED-SPOTTED BLUETHROAT Length 5½ in.

Cyanosylvia svecica

Migrant

A Robin-like bird with rufous sides to base of tail. Male in summer has bright blue gorget bordered black and rufous. This gorget also has rufous central patch. Female has whitish bib bordered speckly black. A migrant, found chiefly on the east coast and in the northern isles.

Family *LANIIDAE*. Shrikes

RED-BACKED SHRIKE Length 6¾ in.

Lanius cristatus End April–Beginning October

This summer visitor is well named " Butcher Bird ", as it butchers birds, mice and insects, and impales them on thorns and spikes. The head and rump of the male are grey, the back chestnut. The black tail is white at the sides, the ear-coverts black, the underparts pinkish-white. The female lacks the grey and black, and is red-brown above and light buff with grey crescent markings beneath.

HAUNT. Hedgerows, telegraph-wires, bushes and trees.

NEST. Of rootlets, grass, moss and wool ; in a bush or hedge.

EGGS. 4 to 6, variable ; pale greyish-buff or pink, with rufous or grey blotches usually at the large end. May or June.

FOOD. Small birds, fledglings, mice, lizards, frogs and large insects.

NOTES. Harsh " chack " and quiet warbling song.

GREAT GREY SHRIKE Length 9½ in.

Lanius excubitor Autumn and winter visitor

This large, uncommon Shrike is a winter visitor. The plumage is soft grey above and almost white beneath ; the wings and tail are black and white. The ear-coverts and a line above the bill are black, as with the Red-backed Shrike. For habits and food, see above.

Family *PRUNELLIDAE*. Accentors

HEDGE SPARROW   Length 5¾ in.

Prunella modularis   Resident

This quiet, brown, insect-eating bird is misnamed "Sparrow", as it is no relation of the House Sparrow or Tree Sparrow, and is a most harmless and useful little bird, correctly named Hedge Accentor, and also called Dunnock. The sexes are alike. The plumage is striated brown above and sombre slate-grey beneath. The bird has a quiet, mouse-like way of creeping about under bushes and herbage in search of insects.

HAUNT. Very general.

NEST. Of moss, wool, grass and hair ; in a bush or hedge, or in a brushwood or faggot pile.

EGGS. 4 or 5, bright turquoise-blue. March–June.

FOOD. Chiefly caterpillars, grubs, spiders, beetles and other insects; also weed-seeds in winter.

NOTES. The note is a shrill, rather rattling, squeak. The song is sweet, high and clear.

DIPPER

Cinclus cinclus

Length nearly 7 in.

Resident

A bird of rocky streams and rivulets, rather quick and quiet in its ways, but its dark plumage and white breast make it easy to distinguish. It also has a distinctive Wren-like way of dipping and curtseying. The plumage of both sexes is dark brown on the head, shading to very dark grey, almost black, on the upper parts. The throat and breast are white, the belly chestnut, shading to black.

HAUNT. Burns, streams and rocky rivers and lakes.

NEST. Of moss and leaves, and sometimes grass; domed, with the entrance hole low down at the side; in a cleft or hole in a rock, bridge or bank.

EGGS. 4 to 6, white. April–June.

FOOD. Aquatic insects and their larvae, watersnails and fry. It dives and swims, using its wings under water.

NOTES. A short " sip, sip ". The song is sweet and trilling.

Family *HIRUNDINIDAE*. Swallows

HOUSE MARTIN
Delichon urbica

Length 5 in.

April–End October

The House Martin is a summer visitor like the Swallow, but it differs from that bird in being black above with a very noticeable white rump, and white beneath from chin to tail. The black, forked tail is shorter than that of the Swallow and lacks the long outer feathers. The feet are covered with white down.

HAUNT. General. Anywhere in the air, and round houses and other buildings.

NEST. Cleverly constructed of mud, with a small entrance hole, under the eaves of a building or similar place.

EGGS. 4 or 5, rather narrow, white. June–August.

FOOD. Insects, chiefly caught when on the wing.

NOTES. It has a twittering note and a similar twittering song.

Family *HIRUNDINIDAE*. Swallows

SAND MARTIN Length 4¾ in.

Riparia riparia March–End September

This summer visitor is the smallest of the Swallow family. It may be distinguished from the Swallow by its dark brown upper parts and small size, and from the House Martin by the absence of the latter's conspicuous white rump and lower back. There is a dark brown band across the breast; the rest of the underparts are white.

HAUNT. Chiefly sandpits, sandy cliffs and river banks, where it breeds with others.

NEST. The Sand Martins nest in colonies, and the top of a sandy cliff or the side of a sandpit may be seen riddled with their holes. The nesting tunnel is a foot or more long, with the nest of hay and feathers, at the far end.

EGGS. 4 or 5, white, narrow. May–July.

FOOD. Insects.

NOTES. Very continuous twitterings.

Family *HIRUNDINIDAE*. Swallows

SWALLOW Length 7½ in.
Hirundo rustica April–October inclusive

The Swallow is one of our best-known and loved summer visitors, much favoured of the poets. It may be distinguished from the other members of the family by the blue sheen on the back and wings, and the long, forked tail. The throat is dull chestnut with a dark blue band below it. The forehead is also dark chestnut. The length includes the long tail feathers.

HAUNT. Very general. Often to be seen skimming low over a pond, or flying with speed and grace in any open space.

NEST. Of mud, grass and feathers, rather open and saucer-shaped ; usually on a beam in a barn, or similar position.

EGGS. 4 to 6, white, spotted with brown, rather long and narrow. May–August.

FOOD. Insects, chiefly flies caught on the wing.

NOTES. A high, slightly metallic " t-weet ", and a twittering song uttered on the wing or from a telegraph wire or other vantage point.

Family *MUSCICAPIDAE*. Flycatchers

SPOTTED FLYCATCHER   Length 5½ in.

Muscicapa striata   End April–End September

This quick, quiet little summer visitor is most interesting to watch. Its plumage is inconspicuous, and when it is sitting very still on the top of its favourite stick or stone, in lee of a wall or herbaceous border, it is not noticeable. But it is constantly darting out from its perch after a passing insect, twisting and

turning in the air so quickly as to confuse any fly. The upper parts are light grey-brown, the underparts nearly white.

HAUNT. Woods, copses, lanes and gardens.

NEST. Chiefly of moss and grass ; in creepers, on a beam, or in a hole in a wall.

EGGS. 4 or 5, nearly white, with light red spots. May–July.

FOOD. Insects, chiefly flies.

NOTES. A high squeak, like a wheelbarrow with a rusty wheel, and a scolding " wee-tuc-tuc ". The song is low and scrapy.

99

Family *MUSCICAPIDAE*. Flycatchers

PIED FLYCATCHER

Length 5 in.

Muscicapa hypoleuca   End April–September

A lively little black and white bird, a summer visitor to wooded areas in parts of Wales, west and north England and south Scotland. Elsewhere it is seen chiefly on migration. The male in summer is black with large white wing-bars, forehead-spot, tail-edges and underparts. The female and autumn male are brown and white with smaller wing-bars. The nest is in a hole in a tree, wall or nest-box, the eggs pale blue.

RED-BREASTED FLYCATCHER

Length 4½ in.

Muscicapa parva   Migrant

A tiny bird rather like a miniature Robin, sometimes seen on migration near the coast. It is light grey-brown above, and whitish beneath with showy white patches on each side of the blackish tail, which is frequently cocked up. Only adult male has scarlet bib and grey head. Occurs usually in autumn in immature or female plumage.

Family *TROGLODYTIDAE.* Wrens

WREN

Troglodytes troglodytes

Length 3¾ in.

Resident

The Wren is one of our smallest birds, and is quite unmistakable with its brown plumage, round-about appearance and tilted-up tail. It also has a mouse-like way of creeping about among the branches in a bush.

HAUNT. Very general, especially in copses and gardens.

NEST. A beautifully constructed domed nest of moss, leaves, grass, wool and feathers, with a round entrance hole at the side ; in a bank, wall, wood-stack or bush.

EGGS. 5 to 12, white, faintly speckled with red-brown. April–June.

FOOD. Caterpillars, spiders and all kinds of insects.

NOTES. A loud, scolding " chur-r-r ", or (when not so annoyed by the intruder) a sharp " tit, tit ". The song is very loud for so small a bird. It is clear and sweet, and full of penetrating and jubilant trills.

GREEN WOODPECKER
Picus viridis

Length 12½ in.

Resident

This beautiful bird with its laughing call-note is interesting to watch as it creeps up the trunk of a tree, tapping the bark and removing insects from the crevices. The plumage is green above, paler beneath, with yellow rump and crimson crown and nape.

HAUNT. Woods, parks and gardens or in trees anywhere.

NEST. A hole in a tree, usually tunnelled in decayed wood.

EGGS. 4 to 7, white. April or May.

FOOD. Chiefly insects. A great many grubs, beetles and other insects which damage trees are eaten. When insect food is short it may take to nuts, berries and fruit. It is especially fond of ants, and will leave the trees in search of ants' nests. It licks up insects on the tip of its long, quick tongue.

NOTES. A loud echoing laugh, " ha-ha-ha-ha " or " plue-plue-plue ".

GREAT SPOTTED WOODPECKER
or PIED WOODPECKER   Length 9 in.

Dendrocopos major   Resident

A handsome bird, better named "Pied Woodpecker", may be distinguished from the smaller "Barred Woodpecker" by its large, conspicuous white "shoulder" patches which show in flight and also as the bird creeps up the trunk of a tree. The plumage is black and white above and creamy-white beneath, shading to crimson on the abdomen and under the tail. The female has no red nape patch. The young have red crowns.

HAUNT.   Among trees.

NEST.   A hole in a tree.

EGGS.   4 to 7, creamy-white.   May.

FOOD.   Insects and their larvae, chiefly those which damage trees.   When insects fail it will eat nuts and berries.

NOTES.   A sharp, scolding "quick, quick", and for "call-note" a fast, vibrating drumming with the bill on a resonant branch, which may be heard from a considerable distance.

LESSER SPOTTED WOODPECKER
or BARRED WOODPECKER   Length 5¾ in.

Dendrocopos minor   Resident

This tiny Woodpecker resembles the Great Spotted Woodpecker in general colouring. It may be distinguished by its small size and by the bands of black and white across the back and wings, which may be seen as it creeps up the trunk of a tree. In addition the male has a red crown.

HAUNT. Among trees.

NEST.   A hole is excavated in a tree.

EGGS.   4 to 8, white.   May.

FOOD.   Chiefly insects and larvae.   Like all the Woodpeckers, it is useful in devouring tree pests.

NOTES.   " Cheek-cheek-cheek ", rather like those of the last species.   It also drums on the branch of a tree with its bill.

Family *PICIDAE*. Woodpeckers

WRYNECK Length 6½ in.

Jynx torquilla Beginning April–Mid-September

The Wryneck is a summer visitor, mostly seen in south-east England. The plumage is brown and grey-brown above, handsomely marked, and the underparts buff, finely barred with brown. The sexes are alike. Its name indicates its habit of twisting the head round to strange angles.

HAUNT. Woods and parks, but it has become very scarce.

NEST. The nesting hole, which is not excavated by the bird itself, may be in a tree or wall, or sometimes in a bank.

EGGS. 6 to 10, white. April or May.

FOOD. Insects and their larvae. It has two of the characteristics of the Green Woodpecker : its long, sticky tongue, which it darts out to catch insects, and its partiality for ants.

NOTES. A loud, ringing, but peevish " quee-quee-quee-quee ", emphatic rather than fast.

Family *CUCULIDAE*. Cuckoos

CUCKOO
Cuculus canorus

Length 13 in.

April–September inclusive

Apart from its popularity as herald of spring, the Cuckoo is not admirable, being polyandrous and a parasite, without care for its young. The plumage is slate-grey above and on the throat and the white underparts are strongly barred. The sexes are similar. The young may be grey-brown, or red-brown heavily barred, as is a rare red form of female.

HAUNT. All parts of the country.

EGGS. These vary, and the Cuckoo lays an egg in the nest of a species with a similar type. The Cuckoo is believed to lay, usually, about 10 or 12 eggs, but as many as 25 have been recorded. They are all laid in different nests. When the young Cuckoo is hatched, it turns out all the other fledglings (or eggs), and they are left to perish on the ground.

FOOD. Many kinds of insects and caterpillars.

NOTES. Besides the well-known " cuckoo ", there are low, harsh calls like coughing or clearing the throat. The female has a long, liquid bubbling call.

Family *APODIDAE*. Swifts

SWIFT   Length 6½ in.

Apus apus   End April–September

This rather Martin-like summer visitor, with its unmistakable scream and long, narrow, curved wings, is easily distinguished as it twists and glides, sometimes at a great height, with its wings rigid or with a few quick wing-beats. The plumage is very dark brown, nearly black, with a light patch on the chin.

HAUNT. The sky, anywhere, even over London.

NEST. Of straw or dry grass and feathers, stuck together with saliva from the bird's mouth ; in a crevice in masonry or a tree, or under a tile, or on a beam in the roof of a building.

EGGS. 2 or 3, white, rather long. May, June.

FOOD. Insects, caught on the wing.

NOTES. A high screaming " chee-ree-eee ". This is particularly noticeable when, as is usually the case, a number of these birds are gliding and turning overhead.

Family *CAPRIMULGIDAE*.   Nightjars

NIGHTJAR or GOATSUCKER   Length 10½ in.

May–September inclusive

Caprimulgus europaeus

This strange bird is more often heard than seen, as its plumage tones with the heath-clad or stony ground on which it is concealed during the day. It sings usually at dusk or after dark, crouched upon a branch, railing or post. The plumage is grey, barred and striated with chestnut, buff and black. The male has white spots on the wings and white tips to the outer tail-feathers.

HAUNT. Heaths and heathery woods.

NEST. There is no nest; the eggs are laid on the ground.

EGGS. 2, long and white, with brown and grey blotches. May, June.

FOOD. Insects, chiefly moths and beetles which fly at dusk.

NOTES. A purring sound like a sewing-machine working, sometimes continuing without a pause for a minute or two. The bird is a summer visitor.

HOOPOE

Length 11 in.

Upupa epops

Migrant

The Hoopoe is seen chiefly on migration in spring near our south and east coasts. In times past, its visits usually ended in a glass case, but it has succeeded in breeding occasionally in south England. It is a most striking bird with its cinnamon-pink plumage, which is barred across  the wings, lower back and tail, with black and white. It has a large, cinnamon, cockatoo-like crest, tipped with black, which is raised in excitement, and a long, thin, slightly curved bill. The wings are broad and rounded and the bird in flight looks like a great butterfly flitting lightly by.

FOOD. All kinds of insects and grubs; worms, woodlice, centipedes, etc.

NOTES. The usual note, which may be heard from a distance, is a hollow-sounding, pipe-like " hoop, hoop, hoop ".

Family *ALCEDINIDAE*. Kingfishers

KINGFISHER
Alcedo atthis

Length 6½ in.

Resident

This gem among birds is so brightly coloured as almost to dazzle the eye in certain lights. I have seen one on the wing looking like a bright blue light rather than anything solid. In another light the bird appeared comparatively dark. The upper parts are vivid blue with a greenish gloss on the crown and wings. The underparts and ear-coverts are chestnut-red, and the chin and a patch on each side of the neck are white.

HAUNT. Lakes, rivers, streams and sometimes the coast.

NEST. The nesting-hole, which is about a yard long, is usually in a sandy river bank. At the end of the tunnel the nesting-chamber contains dry fishbones on which the eggs are laid.

EGGS. 6 to 8, white, rather round. April–June.

FOOD. Water insects and shellfish, tadpoles and small fish.

NOTES. A sharp whistle and a warbling song.

BARN OWL
Tyto alba

Length 13½ in.

Resident

When on the wing the Barn Owl deceives the eye, and often appears to be all white, especially when seen at dusk. The plumage is sandy above, covered with grey markings and small white dots; underneath it is white with a few grey specks. The legs and feet are covered with fur-like white feathers.

HAUNT. Barns, towers, ruins, woods and farm buildings. By day it usually remains hidden.

NEST. There is no nest, except a few odd feathers and some disgorged pellets, the eggs being laid on a ledge in a barn or one of the bird's other haunts.

EGGS. 3 to 8, white. There are a few days between the laying of each egg, and they hatch at different times, so that there are young of different ages, and eggs, in the nest together. The nesting period is variable, usually starting in April.

FOOD. Rats, moles, all kinds of mice, small birds and beetles. (Fish have occasionally been recorded.)

NOTES. Screeches, hisses and snores.

LITTLE OWL
Athene noctua

Length 8½ in.
Resident

This fierce little foreigner was introduced at the end of the last century, and has quickly increased and spread nearly all over England and Wales. Though so small, it will kill birds as large as itself, but feeds chiefly on mammals and insects. The plumage is greybrown, spotted and barred with white, and its small size distinguishes it from other Owls.

HAUNT.   Fairly general, chiefly in woods.

NEST.   The nesting material is almost nil; in a hole in a tree.

EGGS.   4 to 6, white, April or May.

FOOD.   Mainly insects, worms, rodents and birds.

NOTES.   A mewing note, a snore, and also a short, plaintive, repeated whistle.

SHORT-EARED OWL   Length 15 in.
Asio flammeus   Resident

The Short-eared Owl differs from the Long-eared Owl in having very short " ears ". These feathery tufts have not really anything to do with the ears. The Owls have ears at the sides of their heads, concealed by the feathers, as have other birds. The plumage is buff, striated and barred with dark brown. The bird hunts by day as well as at dusk.

HAUNT. Open country. It is not so abundant as other Owls, though fairly common in winter.

NEST. Almost nil ; on the ground in heather or sedge. It seldom nests in south England.

EGGS. 4 to 8, white. March–May.

FOOD. Voles and mice of all kinds, small birds and beetles.

NOTES. A harsh scream and a short bark.

LONG-EARED OWL

Asio otus

Length 14 in.

Resident

This quiet, very uncommon bird hides away by day like most other Owls. The plumage is buff, streaked on the underparts with dark brown, and closely marked on the upper parts with grey and brown. The " ear-tufts ", as they are called, are long and brownish.

HAUNT. Woods, especially fir-woods.

NEST. The Long-eared Owl uses the old nest of a Pigeon, Magpie, Crow, Hawk, or a similar nest.

EGGS. 4 or 5, white.   March or April.

FOOD. Small birds, mice, immature birds and insects.

NOTES.   There is a barking or yapping note, and a longer wavering one, not so distinctive as the long, eerie call of the Wood Owl.

TAWNY or WOOD OWL

Strix aluco

Length 15 in.

Resident

The Tawny Owl is our most familiar Owl with the exception of the Barn Owl, from which it greatly differs in plumage and habitat. Unlike the Barn Owl, it is a woodland bird rather than a frequenter of farm-buildings and towers. The plumage is r i c h b r o w n , handsomely marked w i t h light and d a r k bars and streaks. It is variable in shade, and some birds have a more grey tone.   As with other Owls, the female is a little larger than the male.

HAUNT.   General, especially among trees.

NEST.   Of decayed wood - dust, pellets, and feathers, in a hole in a tree or ruin, or similar place, or in the old nest of a Crow or Pigeon or some other large bird.

EGGS.   3 or 4, white.   (For other details, see Barn-Owl.)

FOOD.   Rats, mice, small birds, young game, rabbits, insects, and even, it is said, fish occasionally.

NOTES.   " Tu-whit ", " whit ", and the well-known long, wavering, eerie call, " ho-hoo-hoo-ooooo ".

Family *FALCONIDAE*.   Harriers, Eagles,
Buzzards, Kites, Hawks and Falcons

GOLDEN EAGLE

Length 32 in. (Male)

Aquila chrysaëtus   Resident

This great bird, with its magnificent flight, is
seldom seen except in north Scotland, where it
still breeds.   The plumage is dark brown, with
golden-brown on the head and nape.   The
feathers on the legs distinguish it from the Sea-
Eagle.   Immature birds have white basal-half of
tail (see illustration) and a conspicuous white patch
at base of primaries.   The female is 3 in. longer
than the male.

H A U N T.   Mountains, crags and wooded highlands in north Scotland.

N E S T.   A large nest is made of branches, sticks,
heather and grass ; on a crag or, rarely, in a tree.

E G G S.   Usually 2, whitish, blotched all over
with red-brown.   March or April.

F O O D.   Rabbits, hares, rats, grouse, small
lambs and carrion.

N O T E S   A shrill yelp or bark

Family *FALCONIDAE*. Harriers, Eagles, Buzzards, Kites, Hawks and Falcons

KITE
Length 24 in.

Milvus milvus
Resident

The Kite is now only found in part of Wales, except for stray appearances elsewhere. It is a fine sight when on the wing, soaring and gliding, and showing the dark undersides of the wings, each ending in a large white " blaze " and black primary - tips. Above, the plumage is red-brown, and the deeply forked tail is chestnut, as are the underparts. The head of adult birds is very pale.

HAUNT. Hilly, wooded country.

NEST. Of sticks, etc., usually an old one.

EGGS. Usually 3. Whitish with dark blotches.

FOOD. Rodents, birds, carrion, frogs, worms.

NOTES. A high, mewing call, and others.

WHITE-TAILED or SEA-EAGLE
Length 27–36 in.

Haliaeëtus albicilla
Rare visitor

This great bird, with wing-span of 8 feet, differs from the Golden Eagle in having a rather short, wedge-shaped tail, which, after the 6th year, is white. A rare visitor to our coasts.

Family *FALCONIDAE*. Harriers, Eagles, Buzzards, Kites, Hawks and Falcons

BUZZARD

Buteo buteo

Length 20 in.(Male)

Resident

Easily recognised by its mewing cry, large size and broad, blunt, moth-like wings, as it circles and glides overhead. The female is 2 in. longer than the male. The plumage is dark brown, lighter beneath and variable. Pale individuals occur. Feet and legs, yellow.

HAUNT. Moors, cliffs, woods and hilly country.

NEST. Of sticks, leaves, grass and wool; on a cliff ledge or in the top of a tree.

EGGS. 2 or 3, slightly greenish-white, blotched with light brown. May.

FOOD. Mice, rats, young rabbits and birds, reptiles and large insects.

NOTES. A loud mewing call, " mee-oo ".

ROUGH-LEGGED BUZZARD

Length 20–24 in.

Buteo lagopus

Winter visitor

A winter visitor chiefly to N. and E. British coasts, marshes, wastes and hills. The upper parts are brown, the head and breast white streaked with brown, the belly very dark, the tail white with a black tip. Silvery underside of wing has black patch at the crook and black-tipped primaries. Legs feathered down to toes. Otherwise like above, with similar mewing cry.

Family *FALCONIDAE*. Harriers, Eagles, Buzzards, Kites, Hawks and Falcons

OSPREY

Pandion haliaëtus

Length 20–23 in.

Chiefly migrant

A magnificent bird with long, angular wings, also called Fish-Hawk, or, in error, Sea Eagle. Contrasting dark brown above and white beneath, white head with blackish band leading from eye down each side of white neck. Silvery-white underside of wing shows a black patch at the front angle. Scarce migrant usually to east coast. Used to breed in Scotland where it still attempts to nest, and recently succeeded.

HAUNT. Near water, fresh or salt, where it may be seen plunging and catching fish with the claws.

NEST. Of sticks, etc., on a tree or ledge of rock or ruin.

EGGS. Usually 3, with bold, dark blotches. April or May.

FOOD. Chiefly fish snatched from water with the feet.

NOTES. Usually high, chick-like piping.

Family *FALCONIDAE*. Harriers, Eagles,
Buzzards, Kites, Hawks and Falcons

MONTAGU'S HARRIER

Circus pygargus

Length 16–18 in.

April–October

Uncommon summer visitor. Male, blue-grey above, and
white, heavily streaked with rust, beneath. Wing-tips and
bar on wing, black. Female, dark brown above, streaked
buff beneath, white band on rump, barred tail.

HEN HARRIER

Circus cyaneus

Length 17–20 in.

Resident and Migrant

Usually uncommon migrant or winter visitor, though
some breed in the North, chiefly Orkney. Differs from
above in plumage of male, i.e., soft-grey with black wing-
tips and white belly and band on rump ; female has
bolder white rump-band than above female.

MARSH HARRIER

Circus aeruginosus

Length 19–22 in.

Summer visitor

The rarest of the three, though a few pairs breed in East
Anglia and the South. Male, brown, with tail and part of
wing light grey, and black wing-tips. Female and young,
dark brown with cream head and shoulders.

Family *FALCONIDAE*. Harriers, Eagles, Buzzards, Kites, Hawks and Falcons

SPARROW HAWK

Accipiter nisus

Length 12 in. (Male)

Resident

This bird of prey catches small birds of many kinds. It skims and dodges and glides low over hedges and copses, suddenly dropping on an unsuspecting victim. The plumage is dark slate-grey above, and whitish beneath tinged with rufous and barred with red-brown. The female is three inches longer than the male, and is a rather browner-grey above, and her white underparts are barred with dark grey. Both birds have a nearly white spot on the back of the neck.

HAUNT. Woods and open country.

NEST. Of sticks, in a tree, or more occasionally on a cliff ledge.

EGGS. 5, nearly white, blotched with red-brown, usually more heavily at one end. May.

FOOD. Chiefly birds, usually small ones ; also mice, frogs, and insects.

NOTES. A short cry, " pew ", " kek, kek, kek ", etc.

Family *FALCONIDAE*.   Harriers, Eagles,
Buzzards, Kites, Hawks and Falcons

KESTREL   Length 13½ in.

Falco tinnunculus   Resident

The Kestrel is
our commonest
Falcon. It may
be seen in the
c o u n t r y any-
where, hovering
in search of prey.
The n a r r o w-
pointed wings,
appearing rather
far forward, are
typical of Hawks
and Falcons, and
when hovering it
displays great
skill in remaining
suspended in the
air, rigid except
for the quivering
wing-tips. The
plumage of the
male is slate-grey
on the head, rump and tail, and light chestnut-brown
on the back, spotted with black. The underparts are
deep buff, spotted and streaked with black. The end
of the tail is black with a white tip. The female is
rufous-brown, striated, and barred across the tail.

HAUNT. Open and wooded country and cliffs

NEST. Of sticks, usually the old nest of a Crow
or other bird, in a tree or on a cliff ledge.

EGGS. 4 or 5, buff, thickly mottled with red-
brown. April or May.

FOOD. Chiefly mice and insects, occasionally
small birds.

NOTES. A short cry repeated " kee, kee, kee " or
" kew, kew ".

Family *FALCONIDAE*. Harriers, Eagles, Buzzards, Kites, Hawks and Falcons

HOBBY
Length 12 in.

Falco subbuteo
April–September

This uncommon Falcon is only a summer visitor, breeding in south England. The plumage is dark slate above, and white, rather tinged with chestnut and streaked with black, beneath, shading to rufous on the thighs and under the tail. There is a heavy black moustache line leading from the black ear-coverts. The flight is dashing, silent and swift, though gliding, wheeling and hovering occur, and remarkable aerobatics in spring display. The female is 2 in. longer than the male.

HAUNT. Chiefly woods and commons.

NEST. The old nest of a Crow or similar bird, which builds in a tree, is used.

EGGS. Usually 3, buff or red-brown, mottled with brown. June.

FOOD. Small birds and insects. Insects are caught with the feet and transferred to the bill.

NOTES. A sharp, repetitive, chattering cry.

Family *FALCONIDAE*.　Harriers, Eagles, Buzzards, Kites, Hawks and Falcons

PEREGRINE FALCON　Length 15 in. (Male)

Falco peregrinus　　　　　　　　　　Resident

This powerful falcon shows great speed and skill in flight, " stooping " on its victim in a headlong rush or overtaking it at speed. T h e plumage is slate-grey above, barred with darker grey, and white barred with black underneath, with a buff tinge on the breast. The top of the head and cheeks are nearly black, with a heavy black moustache-lobe. The female is 3 in. longer than the male.

HAUNT.　The coast: cliffs and mountains.

NEST.　There may be no nesting material used, or only a few sticks; on a precipitous cliff ledge.

EGGS.　2 to 4, red-brown, blotched with darker brown.　April or May.

FOOD.　Sea-birds, waders, pigeons, and others both large and small, and young birds.

NOTES.　A sharp " kek, kek, kek " and others.

Family *FALCONIDAE*. Harriers, Eagles, Buzzards, Kites, Hawks and Falcons

MERLIN
Falco columbarius

Length 11 in. (Male)

Resident

This is the smallest of our Falcons. The plumage of the male is slate-blue above, with darker wing-tips, and the tail has a black band at the tip. The underparts are yellowish-rufous, striated with black. The female is browner, with bars across the tail. She is 1 or 2 in. longer than the male.

HAUNT. Chiefly moorlands in the west and northern half of the British Isles.

NEST. Practically no nesting material is used; the nest is in a slight hollow in the ground in heather or grass, or may be on a cliff.

EGGS. 3 to 5, red-brown and mottled. May.

FOOD. Moorland birds, chiefly small ones, and insects; sometimes small sea-birds. It is swift on the wing and outflies its victim.

NOTES. A chattering scream.

GANNET
Sula bassana

Length 36 or 37 in.

Resident

This great bird has the magnificent wings and flight of a giant Gull, and a wing-span of nearly 6 ft. It can sight a fish from a great height while on the wing, and will drop like an arrow into the water after its prey. The plumage is white with a tinge of buff on the head and neck, and dark brown, almost black, wing-tips. Immatures are first dusky all over, later piebald or white sprinkled with dark spots.

HAUNT. The coast and sea, and at breeding time rocky isles and stacks, chiefly on the north and west of the British Isles.

NEST. Of seaweed and tufts of grass or thrift ; on the rocky ledge of a stack or island in a great colony with others.

EGGS. 1, nearly white, chalky. March or April.

FOOD. Fish.

NOTES. Short and harsh.

Family *PHALACROCORACIDAE*. Cormorants

CORMORANT   Length 36 in.

Phalacrocorax carbo   Resident

Plumage, black and very dark brown, with green and purple sheen ; chin white. In spring there is a white patch across the thigh. Immatures, dark brown, whitish beneath.

HAUNT. The coast, tidal rivers, occasionally inland waters.

NEST. Of seaweed ; with others on rocky cliffs and islands. Sometimes of sticks and grass, inland.

EGGS. 3 to 5, nearly white, chalky. April, May.

FOOD. Fish and eels, which it dives for and overtakes under water.

NOTES. A silent bird, except for an occasional harsh croak.

Family *PHALACROCORACIDAE*. Cormorants

SHAG Length 30 in.
Phalacrocorax aristotelis Resident

The Shag differs from the Cormorant in its smaller size and the lack of white on chin and thighs. The adult bird is a glossy, metallic green. In the spring it wears an erect crest on the head. It is more exclusively a bird of wild, rocky cliffs and islets, especially on the west coast. Immature Shags are brownish, pale beneath, like young Cormorants, but having 12 tail-feathers to the Cormorant's 14.

HAUNT. Rocky coasts.

NEST. Of seaweed; on a cliff or cave ledge.

EGGS. 2 to 5, nearly white, chalky. April–May.

FOOD. Fish, which it catches by diving and swimming under water with great speed and with agile twists and turns.

NOTES. An occasional deep croak.

Family *ANATIDAE*.   Geese, Swans and Ducks

WHOOPER SWAN	Length 6o in.
Cygnus cygnus	Chiefly winter visitor
BEWICK'S SWAN	Length 48 in.
Cygnus columbianus	Winter visitor

Both these wild Swans are winter visitors, the Whooper chiefly to the north and east of Britain, the Bewick's chiefly to Ireland and the north. The plumage is white, the legs nearly black, the bill yellow and black, unlike that of the Mute Swan, which is deep orange with a black knob at the base of the upper mandible. The illustration shows a Whooper. The Bewick's has a shorter, less pointed area of yellow on the bill. Both birds hold the neck erect without the graceful S-curve of that of the Mute.

HAUNT. Salt-water lochs and inlets of the sea ; estuaries and inland waters.

FOOD. Water-weed, shellfish, etc.

NOTES. The Whooper makes clear bugle or trumpeting notes, the Bewick's has less clarion honk-ing.

MUTE SWAN

Length 60 in.

Cygnus olor

Resident

This partly domesticated Swan is familiar to all, on ponds, lakes and rivers. It can be distinguished from the truly wild Swans by its deep orange bill with a black knob and patch at the base, and when excited, by the arched wings when swimming.

NEST. A mass of vegetation and down ; on the ground near water.

EGGS. 5 to 12, greenish-white. April. Both birds are very good parents, guarding the nest with care. The male, who shares in incubating the eggs, will attack an intruder with ferocity. The young are carried on the parents' backs after leaving the nest.

FOOD. Mostly water plants and insects ; also scraps.

NOTES. It has grunting and barking notes and hisses when angry.

Family *ANATIDAE*.   Geese, Swans and Ducks

GREY LAG GOOSE   Length 30–35 in.
Anser anser   Resident

Though mainly a winter visitor and migrant in Britain, it breeds in parts of N. Scotland and N. Isles.   Plumage, grey-brown with light-grey fore-wing ; feet pink, bill orange. Closely resembles farmyard Grey Geese.   Flocks fly in V-formation or lines.

HAUNT.   Moors and marshes in the north ; coasts, estuaries, flats, meadows in winter.

NEST.   Very large ; of heather, sticks, leaves, grass, with down to cover the eggs ; on the ground.

EGGS.   4 to 6, creamy-white.   April.

FOOD.   Grain, grass and other vegetation.

NOTES.   Not unlike those of the farmyard goose, " kark, kark " or " gaggle ".

BEAN GOOSE   Length 28–35 in.
Anser arvensis   Winter visitor

Differs from the last in darker, rather browner plumage, especially on the head and neck ; orange-yellow feet ; orange and black bill, sometimes all-black except for orange band near tip.

Family *ANATIDAE*.　Geese, Swans and Ducks

WHITE-FRONTED GOOSE　Length 26–30 in.
Anser albifrons　　　　　　　　　　Winter visitor

A winter visitor, differing from the Grey Lag chiefly in its smaller size, black patches or bars on the breast, and the white front from forehead to bill.　The plumage is grey-brown with the white stern of all grey geese ; the bill pink, the feet orange.　It is most numerous on the west coast.

LESSER WHITE-FRONTED GOOSE
Anser erythropus　　　　　　　　Length 21–26 in.

Scarce winter visitor, smaller than above, with smaller bill, larger area of white extending to crown, and yellow ring to eye.

PINK-FOOTED GOOSE　Length 24–30 in.
Anser brachyrhychus　　　　　　　　Winter visitor

Often seen in large flocks, most numerous on the east coast.　Head and neck very dark, mantle blue-grey, breast grey-brown, small bill pink and black, feet pink.

Family *ANATIDAE*.   Geese, Swans and Ducks
BRENT GOOSE
Length 22–24 in.

Branta bernicla
Winter visitor

This bird differs from the foregoing grey geese in its black, white and grey plumage and small size.   Dark-bellied form (shown above) chiefly S. and E. coasts, light-grey-bellied form mainly Ireland and W. coasts.

HAUNT.   The seashore and estuaries.

FOOD.   Chiefly sea-grass and weed, also sand-worms.

NOTES.   A low croak.

CANADA GOOSE
Length 36–40 in.

Branta canadensis
Resident

This large and handsome goose was introduced as an ornamental bird on various lakes, but now considerable numbers have become quite wild.   The plumage is light ash-brown, the long neck and crown black, the cheeks white.

HAUNT.   Lakes, broads and parks.

NEST.   A flat mass of vegetation and bits of bark or twig, and a smother of down ; on the ground by water; chiefly in East Anglia, Home Counties and Midlands.

EGGS.   3 to 7, creamy-white.   April and May.

FOOD.   Similar to that of other Geese, including grass.

NOTES.   A " honk ", rather musical when heard from a distance, but clamorous near by.

Family *ANATIDAE*.   Geese, Swans and Ducks

MALLARD or WILD DUCK   Length 23 in.

Anas platyrhynchos   Resident

The Mallard is our best-known wild duck. During the summer moult the grey and wine-brown, with dark bottle-green head and white collar, of the drake's plumage is obscured and brownish. The duck is mottled brown; both have violet, white-bordered wing-bars.

HAUNT.   Fresh water, marshes, estuaries and sometimes the shore.

NEST.   Of grass, vegetation and down; on the ground in herbage by water, marsh, or in a wood; occasionally in a low tree. The duck usually covers the eggs with down and leaves before going away from the nest.

EGGS.   8 to 14, pale green or olive-white.   March–May.

FOOD.   Almost anything: insects, worms, slugs, snails, shellfish, frogs, grain and berries.

NOTES.   "Quark", "dreek" and a soft quacking murmur.

BARNACLE GOOSE   Length 23–27 in.

Branta leucopsis   Winter visitor

Visits chiefly N.W. coasts of Britain.   Handsome black and white plumage: crown, nape, neck and upper breast black; face and forehead white; underparts pale grey; dark grey back barred with lines of black and white; white stern, black tail; small bill and feet black.

Family *ANATIDAE*.   Geese, Swans and Ducks

SHELDUCK   Length 24 in.

Tadorna tadorna   Resident

This handsome marine duck may be recognised by its large size and piebald plumage of green-glossed black, white and rust.   Bill scarlet, legs pink.

HAUNT. The coast, sand-dunes and tidal mud-flats.

NEST. Of bents, moss and down, in a burrow, usually a rabbit's.   This is sometimes at a distance from the coast, and thither the downy black and white ducklings have to walk by devious ways escorted by their anxious parents.   Unfortunately they often meet disaster on the way.

EGGS. 6 to 12, creamy-white.   May.

FOOD. Sand-worms and hoppers, shellfish, snails, crustaceans, seaweed.

NOTES. Soft quacking notes.   The drake has a low whistle.

Family *ANATIDAE*.   Geese, Swans and Ducks

GARGANEY
Anas querquedula

Length 15 in.

March–September

This is a much smaller Duck than the Mallard, and more resembles the Teal in size. It is a summer visitor, breeding mostly in south-east England. The head, back, breast and stern of the drake are brown, shading to red-brown on the cheeks and neck, with a conspicuous white stripe from above the eye to the back of the neck. The underparts and flanks are white and pale grey.   The duck is brown.   Besides quacking, the drake has a clicking, rattling note.

GADWALL
Anas strepera

Length 20 in.

Resident

This is a scarce winter visitor, and a restricted resident breeding here and there in Scotland and N. and S.E. England.   Drake, dull brownish-grey, often with almost slaty flanks and mantle ; black stern. Drake in eclipse and duck, brown.   Both have squarish white wing-patch next to black patch, shown in flight.

Family *ANATIDAE*. Geese, Swans and Ducks

WIGEON   Length 18 in.

Anas penelope   Resident

The Wigeon is chiefly a winter visitor to the
British Isles though resident in north Britain. The
plumage of the drake is yellow on the forehead ;
the head, neck and breast are orange-chestnut,
the back and flanks grey, with a large white patch
on the wing and white on the underparts.   The
duck is brown and mottled.   Like other drakes,
the male Wigeon has an " eclipse " period in
summer when most of the smart characteristics of
his plumage are lost.

H A U N T. Sandy shores, estuaries, meres, lakes.

N E S T.   Of herbage and sooty down ; concealed in vegetation near water.

E G G S.   5 to 10, creamy-white.   April–June.

F O O D.   Water insects, sand-worms, sea-grass,
shellfish, grain and even berries.

NOTES. The drake has a pleasing whistle:
" whee-oo " ; the duck a purring growl.

Family *ANATIDAE*.   Geese, Swans and Ducks

TEAL   Length 14 in.

Anas crecca   Resident

This handsome little Duck, which is commonest in winter, is easily distinguished by the chestnut and metallic green on the head of the drake, and the grey of the body plumage with a long white streak above the wing. The duck is mottled buff and brown. Both birds may be recognised by their small size and green wing-bars. In " eclipse " the drake more resembles the duck.

HAUNT. Lakes and pools; and, in winter, estuaries.

NEST. Of herbage and very dark brownish down; on the ground among rushes or in a wood.

EGGS. 8 to 12, buffish or greenish. May.

FOOD. Water plants and insects, crustaceans and grain.

NOTES. A clear whistle and other conversational notes. The duck also quacks.

Family *ANATIDAE*.　Geese, Swans and Ducks

POCHARD　　　　　　　　　　Length 18 in.
Aythya ferina　　　　　　　　　　Resident

　　Though most numerous in winter, the Pochard
is a resident with us.　The plumage of the drake
is distinctive.　The head and upper part of the
neck are chestnut, the lower part of the neck and
breast are black.　The rest of the plumage is soft
grey, except for black tail-coverts.　In "eclipse"
the plumage is rather browner, barred with grey.
The duck is brownish and more inconspicuous.

　H A U N T　Lakes and broads ; occasionally the
sea.

　N E S T.　Of rushes and other vegetation and
sooty down ; on the ground in herbage near water.

　E G G S.　6 to 12, greenish or yellowish-white.
April–June.

　F O O D.　Chiefly water-weed ; also water-
insects and shellfish, for which it dives.

　N O T E S.　A croaking " quack ".　The drake
also has a soft whistle.

Family *ANATIDAE*.   Geese, Swans and Ducks

SHOVELER   Length 20 in.
Spatula clypeata   Resident

The Shoveler is most common as a bird of
passage, but is also a winter and summer visitor
and resident breeding in small numbers.
The head of the drake is dark bottle-green, the
breast white, the underparts bright chestnut.
The brown and black back has a blue sheen.   The
unusual spade-like bill is noticeable at close
quarters.   The duck is mottled brown.

   H A U N T.   Marshes and ponds.

   N E S T.   Of vegetation or grass and rather sooty
down ; concealed in herbage on the ground.

   E G G S.   8 to 12, greenish-white.   April or
May.

   F O O D.   Chiefly water-insects and weed ;   also
frogs and shellfish.

   N O T E S.   " Quack ", and the flight-note which
is " took " or " tuk, tuk "

Family *ANATIDAE*.   Geese, Swans and Ducks

PINTAIL   Length 22 in.

Anas acuta   Resident

   The Pintail breeds regularly in several localities and is also a winter visitor.   The plumage of the drake is greyish with white underparts.   The head and neck are dark brown with a white stripe leading up the neck, on each side.   The dark tail is long and pointed.   During the " eclipse " in summer the drake is dusky brown.   The duck is mottled and brownish, lighter underneath.   Her tail is less long.

H A U N T.   The sea, and fresh water near the coast.

N E S T.   Of herbage and dark brown down ; on the ground among vegetation.

E G G S.   7 to 10, greenish-yellow.   April or May.

F O O D.   Shellfish, water-weed, sea-grass, crustaceans and grain.

NOTES.   Rather silent.   Sometimes a low whistle or croak.

TUFTED DUCK
Aythya fuligula

Length 17 in.

Resident

This resident diving Duck, with its black and white plumage, has a silky tuft or drooping crest on the head. The male is black, with white flanks and underparts. The female is dark brown, with pale flanks and shorter crest.

HAUNT.   Inland waters ; lakes and meres ; occasionally the shore.

NEST.   Of reeds and other vegetation and rather sooty down ; on the ground near water, concealed in herbage.

EGGS.   8 to 10, olive colour.   May or June.

FOOD.   Water-weed, insects and shellfish.

NOTES.   A grating " currah " and a softer note.

SCAUP
Aythya marila

Length 19 in.

Winter visitor

The Scaup is a winter visitor to our shores, not breeding, except very rarely in Scotland and the Northern Isles.   The drake has a black head, neck, breast, and stern ; grey back and white flanks and underparts.   The duck is brown, shading to nearly white underneath, with a white area round base of bill.

HAUNT.   Round the coast ; rarely inland waters.   It is a good diver.

Family *ANATIDAE*.   Geese, Swans and Ducks

EIDER DUCK   Length 23 in.
Somateria mollissima   Resident

The Eider is resident on the Scottish, N.E. English and N. Irish coasts, and is seen elsewhere as a winter visitor. It is a beautiful and interesting bird. The drake is magnificent in glistening white and velvet-black, with pink-flushed breast and almond-green nape. The duck is mottled brown. With both birds the head and bill form a heavy wedge-shape. She is a devoted mother, seldom leaving eggs and sometimes going without food for 3 or 4 weeks. Commerce has taken advantage of her maternal instincts and the down which she plucks from her body and places in the nest in great profusion has been constantly robbed for eiderdown quilts.

HAUNT.   The sea.

NEST.   Of grass and seaweed and much grey down ; on the ground, in herbage or under a boulder.

EGGS.   4 to 7, pale green.   May–July.

FOOD.   Crustaceans and shellfish.

NOTES.   A grating note and a coo.

GOLDENEYE
Bucephala clangula

Length 18 in. (Drake)
Winter visitor

The Goldeneye, which is only a winter visitor, differs in appearance from the Tufted Duck chiefly in having a white breast, and a round, white patch at the base of the bill, near the eye. The duck, which is 2 in. shorter, lacks this white spot, and is grey with white collar and brown head.

HAUNT. Lakes and the sea. The bird is a fine diver.

SMEW
Mergus albellus

Length 16½ in.
Winter visitor

The Smew is a winter visitor, chiefly on the east coast. The drake is nearly all white, lined with black. There is a black patch from eye to bill and wide black stripes on nape and back; the wings are partly black. In flight the black parts are more noticeable. The duck is grey on the back, with chestnut on the crown and back of the neck. She is only 15 in. long.

HAUNT. The sea, estuaries and inland waters.
FOOD. Fish, crustaceans and water-insects.

Family *ANATIDAE*.   Geese, Swans and Ducks

LONG-TAILED DUCK

Length 20–23 in. (Drake)

Clangula hyemalis   Winter visitor

This bird is a diving-duck.   The plumage of the drake is variable according to the time of year. In winter it is white and brownish-black ; and when seen without full winter dress is browner. The long, thin tail narrowing to two fine points is always characteristic of the drake.   The duck lacks these and is only 16 in. long.   Her plumage above is almost entirely brown.   The length given above includes the long tail-feathers.

H A U N T .   The sea, and occasionally inland waters.

F O O D .   Shellfish and crustaceans, for which it dives, and many kinds of plankton.

N O T E S .   The bird is conversational, and calls constantly by day and night with a musical note, from which it gets its Scottish name of " Calloo ".

Family *ANATIDAE*.   Geese, Swans and Ducks

GOOSANDER   Length 26 in. (Drake)

Mergus merganser   Winter visitor and resident

The Goosander is chiefly a winter visitor to Britain, resident only in Scotland and Northumberland.   The drake is a handsome bird, with glossy green-black head and back, pale salmon-pink underparts and scarlet bill and legs.   The duck, which is 2 in. shorter, has a chestnut head and grey back.   Both sexes have a finely serrated bill, which enables them to hold a slippery fish with ease.

H A U N T.   The sea, estuaries and inland waters.

N E S T.   A little grass or moss and down ; in a hole in a bank, rock or tree.

E G G S.   7 to 12, cream colour.   April or May.

F O O D.   Fish, for which it swims under water ; sometimes it is beneath the surface for nearly two minutes without coming up.

N O T E S.   Harsh and low.

Family *ANATIDAE*.   Geese, Swans and Ducks

RED-BREASTED MERGANSER
Length 23 in. (Drake)

Mergus serrator   Winter visitor and resident

The Merganser is mainly a winter visitor but breeds in Scotland, Cumberland, Anglesey and Ireland.   It has a pronounced crest or tuft on the head, spotted chestnut breast, grey flanks, glossy green-black head and back and white underparts.   The slightly smaller duck is chestnut on the head and neck, and grey on the back.   Both birds have scarlet bills, finely serrated, as are those of the Goosander and Smew.

H A U N T. The sea ; only occasionally inland waters.

N E S T. Of grass or leaves and grey down ; on the ground, concealed in herbage, bushes, or by a boulder.

E G G S. 6 to 12, olive or greyish-buff.   May or June.

F O O D. Mostly fish ; also crustaceans and shell-fish. The bird swims under water.

N O T E S. A grating note and a coo.

Family *ANATIDAE*. Geese, Swans and Ducks

COMMON SCOTER
Melanitta nigra

Length 19 in.
Visitor and resident

This black Duck is a visitor to our coasts, chiefly in winter, and also at other times, resident only in N. Scotland and N. Ireland. The plumage of the drake is black, and the duck is brown with whitish cheeks.

HAUNT. The sea, and occasionally inland lakes or meres.

NEST. Of grass and sooty down, on the ground, concealed in herbage.

EGGS. 5 to 10, buffish-white. End of May or June.

FOOD. Chiefly shellfish ; also crustaceans.

NOTES. A grating call and softer notes between the duck and drake.

VELVET SCOTER
Melanitta fusca

Length 22 in.
Winter visitor

This bird may be distinguished from the common Scoter by the large white bar on the wing of both the black drake and the brown duck. It is a winter visitor to our coasts, most uncommon in the south-west.

Family *PLATALEIDAE*.   Spoonbills and Ibises

SPOONBILL
Platalea leucorodia

Length 34 in.
Migrant

This remarkable bird is chiefly a migrant with us, but it also sometimes winters in the south-west, and occasionally summers. The plumage is white, and adults have a yellowish patch on the upper breast, and in summer a drooping crest. Immature birds are white with blackish wing-tips.  The long, spatulate bill is often swept from side to side while feeding in soft mud and water, and in flight the bill and neck are outstretched, distinguishing the Spoonbill from white egrets or herons when on the wing.

HAUNT.   Estuaries, marshes and shallow pools near the coast.

FOOD.   Parts of water-plants and their seeds, fish and other water animals and insects.

NOTES.   A silent bird, very rarely uttering a low grunt.

Family *ARDEIDAE*.   Herons

BITTERN   Length 30 in.
Botaurus stellaris   Resident

In spite of past persecution, the Bittern is breeding in increasing numbers chiefly in East Anglia in guarded sanctuaries, and also in one or two suitable reed-beds elsewhere. It is also a winter visitor. It is a large handsome heron with warm brown and buff plumage barred with black.

HAUNT.   It is a shy, secretive bird, usually hidden in reed-beds.   When disturbed it sometimes points its bill to the sky and stretches its long neck up in order to become invisible among the reeds.

FOOD.   Like that of the Heron; including fish, eels, frogs and other creatures.

NOTES.   There are various cries, including a low " honk " or " agh ", but the most outstanding note is a deep boom which is the spring call of the male and carries for over a mile.   This is uttered with the bird's bill pointing upward.

Family *ARDEIDAE*.   Herons

HERON

Length 36 in.

Ardea cinerea

Resident

The Heron is a beautiful water-bird, often standing motionless for a long time in shallow water watching for fish and frogs. One which I saw standing in a marsh, with its body hidden in reeds, was almost invisible, the long, snaky neck and thin, wedge-shaped head appearing to be only a whitened branch, until a slight movement betrayed it.  When it takes to its great grey wings with dark tips, the unusually slow and languid wing-beats are distinctive. The usual position when standing is with the head sunk on the shoulders. The head is also drawn back in flight.

H A U N T.   Marshes, woods, rivers, lakes, estuaries and saltings.

N E S T.   Of sticks, very large, usually in a tree, in a colony or heronry ; sometimes in a marsh or on a cliff.

E G G S.   3 to 5, greenish-blue. February or March.

F O O D.   Fish, frogs, eels, insects, water-voles ; and occasionally waterfowl, though nearly always young ones.

N O T E S.   A sonorous " croak ".

Family *BURHINIDAE*

STONE CURLEW	Length 16 in.
Burhinus oedicnemus	March–End October

The Stone Curlew or Thick-knee is a summer visitor, breeding in East Anglia and some southern counties, and rarely wintering here. The plumage is suited for hiding in its favourite surroundings, and it often takes refuge in camouflage rather than flight. It has a horizontal carriage and rather thick legs. The plumage is light reddish-brown, striated with dark brown. The underparts are lighter.

HAUNT. Stony heaths, wastes, downs and wolds.

NEST. A slight hollow in the ground.

EGGS. Usually 2, buff or creamy-grey, marbled and blotched with dark brown. April or May.

FOOD. Chiefly nocturnal insects, worms and snails; rarely frogs and mice. Feeds chiefly at dusk and night.

NOTES. A wild, strange, wailing cry, sometimes sweet and clear, often Curlew-like.

Family *PHALAROPODIDAE*

GREY PHALAROPE

Length 8 in.

Phalaropus fulicarius

Migrant

The Phalaropes differ from other Sandpipers by swimming rather than wading and by having a narrow rim of webbing round the toes.   The Grey Phalarope is a migrant usually seen in autumn, when driven to our southern and south-western shores by gales.   Winter plumage, usually seen with us : grey above, white beneath, whitish head with dark mark through eye. In summer : chestnut-red beneath, dark brown above, white cheeks.

RED-NECKED PHALAROPE

Length 7 in.

Phalaropus lobatus

May–August

An occasional migrant, chiefly in autumn.   To a few Scottish isles and part of N.W. Ireland it is a summer visitor, breeding near water or marsh on the ground, usually in June.   The plumage in winter is grey above, streaked, with dark mark through eye; underparts white.   Distinguished from Grey Phalarope by very thin bill.   In summer, dark grey with orange-chestnut on sides of neck and head, and white beneath and on the cheeks and throat.

Family *RECURVIROSTRIDAE*. Avocets and Stilts

AVOCET

Recurvirostra avosetta

Length 17 in.

Summer visitor

A most graceful white wader with black bands crossing the back and wings, and black on the crown continuing down the nape, black wingtips, and a long, very thin, upcurved black bill, which is, perhaps, this bird's most remarkable feature. In spite of the black markings mentioned, it still remains a glistening white bird when seen from a distance, its slender form supported on long, lead-blue legs. This bird, for a century lost to us except as a rare migrant, has, since 1946, re-established itself as a summer visitor breeding near the Suffolk coast in some numbers. It has also, occasionally, bred elsewhere, but is usually a migrant and winter visitor, chiefly to S. and S.W. England.

HAUNT. Estuaries, salt-marshes, etc.

NEST. A slight hollow, often unlined, on mud or sand, in a colony.

EGGS. Usually 4. Pale putty or buff, spotted black.

FOOD. Insects, larvae, molluscs, shrimps, fry.

NOTES. " Kloo-it ", and clamour if disturbed at colony.

WOODCOCK
Length 13½ in.

Scolopax rusticola
Resident

The Woodcock, unfortunately for itself, is very much a game bird. The plumage is a wonderfully finely marked combination of browns, barred with black and chestnut. The rather long, thin bill and high forehead are distinctive. By day it is secretive and usually remains under cover.

HAUNT. Woods, marshes, ditches and copses.

NEST. Practically no nesting material is used, the nest being a slight hollow in the ground, usually in a wood.

EGGS. 4, creamy-white, blotched with light brown and grey. March or April.

FOOD. Chiefly worms; also insects.

NOTES. In the display flight at dusk, known as " roding ", the male makes a low croaking sound and a thin " zwick ".

COMMON SNIPE
Gallinago gallinago

Length 10½ in.

Resident

By day the Snipe usually remains hidden in a marsh, but when disturbed it flies in erratic zigzags until out of gunshot. The plumage is patterned with various shades of dark and light brown, with conspicuous stripes on crown and back.

HAUNT. Marshes and moors.

NEST. Of grass ; on the ground, concealed in rushes, long grass or other herbage.

EGGS. 4, pale olive, blotched with brown. April.

FOOD. Chiefly worms ; also various insects.

NOTES. Alarm- and flight-note is a grating, harsh splutter. In spring, a mechanical " chip-per, chip-per, chip-per " is heard. It has a clicking, wooden tone which sounds alternately near and far away. In display-flight, a bleating (" drumming ") is made with the tail and wings.

KNOT   Length 10 in.

Calidris canutus   Winter visitor

This wader is a winter visitor to our shores, often in large numbers. In winter plumage it is grey above and whitish beneath. Immature birds are browner, and birds which appear in summer, as a few may, are chestnut-red on the head and underparts.

H A U N T. Sandy shores and mud-flats.

F O O D. Sandworms, shellfish and crustaceans.

N O T E S. " Knot " or " knut ".

JACK SNIPE   Length 7½ in.

Lymnocryptes minimus   Winter visitor

The Jack Snipe is only a winter visitor. The plumage is very like that of the common Snipe, but it may be distinguished by its smaller size. The flight is less noticeably zigzag, and when disturbed the bird quickly takes cover again. In other respects it closely resembles the larger bird.

Family *SCOLOPACIDAE*

PURPLE SANDPIPER
Calidris maritima

Length 8¼ in.

Winter visitor

This wader differs in its haunts from most of the others, which favour sandy stretches and mud-flats. It frequents the rocky coast, and consorts with the larger Turnstone on seaweed-covered boulders. It is an autumn and winter visitor, non-breeding birds occasionally staying through the summer. The plumage is very dark blackish-brown, mottled with chestnut and paler edgings ; and in winter almost entirely dusky above with a purple sheen. There is some white on the underparts and beneath the wings. The legs are yellow.

LITTLE STINT
Calidris minuta

Length 5¼ in.

Migrant

The smallest of the waders, like tiny Dunlin with straight bill shorter than Dunlin's. Summer plumage : mottled red-brown on breast and upper parts, white beneath. In winter, greyer, whitish on face and underparts. Usually shows light streaks on back forming V. Often seen on migration with Dunlins or other small waders, usually in autumn.

Family *SCOLOPACIDAE*

DUNLIN   Length 7 in.
Calidris alpina   Resident and visitor

The Dunlin is our most abundant wader. It breeds in Scotland and sparingly in England, Wales and Ireland. The plumage is variable ; but, roughly speaking, in winter it is grey on the upper parts and breast, and white beneath, and in summer, red-brown above with a large black patch on the lower breast.

HAUNT. Sandy shores, estuaries, mud-flats and salt marshes. It is a summer and winter visitor and an abundant migrant.

NEST. Of grass, usually on a moor.

EGGS. 4, buff or pale green, blotched with brown. May or June.

FOOD. Insects and larvae, sandhoppers, sand-worms and small crustaceans. It swims, as well as wades, in search of food.

NOTES. Alarm- and flight-note, a shrill, split pipe; and from feeding flocks, a soft twitter which is music to lovers of the flats.

Family *SCOLOPACIDAE*

SANDERLING
Crocethia alba

Length 8 in.

Migrant and winter visitor

The Sanderling is one of our most dainty waders. It is a bird of passage and is seen in greatest numbers in spring and autumn, but it also winters with us, and a few non-breeding birds remain through the summer. Like the Dunlin it is gregarious, and may be seen with Ringed-Plover, Knots and other waders. On the sands it is energetic and runs at great speed, its legs moving faster than the eye can see, as it chases sandhoppers and other insects. The plumage is whiter than that of other waders. In winter it is pale grey above and white beneath. In summer dress the grey is exchanged for mottled chestnut or golden-brown.

HAUNT. Usually sandy shores.

FOOD. Sandhoppers, sandworms, shellfish and seaweed.

NOTES. "Whit, whit"—a musical twitter as a little flock takes to its wings and makes a short flight to the next stretch of sand.

Family *SCOLOPACIDAE*

CURLEW SANDPIPER
Calidris testacea

Length 7½ in.

Passage migrant

The Curlew-Sandpiper is so called because the end of its long bill has a slight downward curve, though not so much as that of the Curlew. It is only a bird of passage with us, most usually seen in spring and autumn. It is not unlike the Dunlin in appearance, but may be distinguished in flight by its white rump. In spring and summer the plumage is mottled chestnut, black and grey, with warm chestnut underparts. In winter the back is grey-brown and the underparts white.

HAUNT. Mud-flats and saltings, and sometimes sewage farms.

FOOD. The food consists of the usual marine creatures, including sandworms, hoppers and molluscs ; and inland, insects and freshwater shellfish.

NOTES. Low twitters and a flight-note : " twer-ret " or " chirrip ".

Family *SCOLOPACIDAE*

RUFF   Length 12 in. (Male)

Philomachus pugnax   Passage migrant

The Ruff has suffered persecution and is now only a migrant, seen chiefly in spring and autumn. It is a remarkable bird with greatly varying plumage. The ruff and ear-tufts of the male are worn only in spring and vary in colour. They may be red, yellow, black or white, barred or plain, and are extended in display. At other times of the year the plumage resembles that of the Reeve (female). She is 2½ in. shorter and her plumage is mottled grey-brown shading to white beneath. The colour of the legs varies from grey-green to bright yellow or orange. In flight an oval white patch is seen on each side of the tail.

HAUNT. The seashore, sewage farms, swamps, marshes and lakes.

FOOD. Chiefly insects and worms.

NOTES. An occasional double pipe ; but it is not a talkative bird.

Family *SCOLOPACIDAE*

REDSHANK
Length 11 in.

Tringa totanus
Resident

This is one of our more familiar waders, with long orange-scarlet legs. In the summer the plumage is streaky brown above, and whitish beneath, barred and speckled with brown. There is white on the rump and a broad white band along the fringe of the wing. In winter, the plumage is a greyer brown above and rather whiter beneath.

HAUNT. The shore, tidal mud-flats, marshes, sewage farms, meres and broads. It is quick to take alarm and to fly round piping anxiously.

NEST. Of grass, in a marsh, or similar place; often concealed by grass or herbage which is trained over to screen it

EGGS. 4, yellowish-buff, spotted with dark brown. March or April.

FOOD. Insects, shellfish and crustaceans, for which it swims as well as wades.

NOTES. A clear " tu-yu-yu ", or " tew ", or shrill, scolding " t-keep, t-keep ", and others.

SPOTTED or DUSKY REDSHANK
Length 12 in.

Tringa erythropus
Migrant

An uncommon migrant with blackish summer plumage. Bill and legs longer than Redshank's, with legs darker red in summer, and winter plumage greyer and whiter. Also lacks Redshank's white fringe to wing seen in flight. Flight-note " chewit ".

Family *SCOLOPACIDAE*

GREENSHANK

Tringa nebularia

Length 12 in.

Chiefly migrant

The Greenshank is a bird of passage with us, only staying to nest in north Scotland. It consorts with Redshanks and other waders. The olive-green legs distinguish it from the Redshank, as well as the very slight upward curve of the bill, and the whiter head, neck and underparts. In summer the back is dark brown, the head and neck spotted with brown. In winter it is greyer and whiter. In flight, the unbarred wings and white rump are distinctive.

HAUNT. The shore, mud-flats, marshes, meres and sewage farms.

NEST. By a marsh or other water, usually concealed in rushes.

EGGS. 4, cream or buff, blotched with grey or brown. May.

FOOD. Worms, insects, tiny fish and sand eels, shellfish and crustaceans.

NOTES. Alarm- and flight-note, a loud, anxious " tew, tew, tew ". Other clear notes at breeding place.

Family *SCOLOPACIDAE*

GREEN SANDPIPER	Length 9 in.
Tringa ochropus	Passage migrant
WOOD SANDPIPER	Length 8 in.
Tringa glareola	Passage migrant

These two migrants are seen in spring and autumn, chiefly in autumn, especially the Wood Sandpiper. Both may be distinguished from the Common Sandpiper by white rumps and brown, unbarred wings. The wings of the Green are much darker and look blackish in flight, on the undersurface as well as above. The legs of the Wood Sandpiper are lighter and usually yellowish.

HAUNT. Marshes and marsh-pools, and the margins of lakes, rivers and dykes.

FOOD. Like that of other waders, including molluscs, insects and other aquatic creatures.

NOTES. Green Sandpiper, clear " klee-weet ", or " kli-weet-a-weet " ; Wood-Sandpiper, sharp " chip, chip, chip " or soft " chirrif ".

Family *SCOLOPACIDAE*

COMMON SANDPIPER
Length 7¾ in.

Tringa hypoleucos
April–October

This quietly dressed but attractive wader is a summer visitor, breeding chiefly in the hills of Scotland, Ireland, Wales and northern England, but is a common migrant to all parts of the British Isles. The plumage is olive-brown above and on the breast, and white underneath. When standing, it has a habit of nodding the head and swaying the hind parts up and down.

HAUNT. Clear trout streams in the hills; and, on migration, rivers, lakes and coast.

NEST. Of a little grass or other herbage; on the ground, usually near water, concealed in bushes or vegetation.

EGGS. 4, buff, spotted with brown. May.

FOOD. Insects and their larvae, worms and crustaceans.

NOTES. Shrill, high "peep" or "twee" repeated. Song, a rippling repetition of " Kitti-needie ".

Family *SCOLOPACIDAE*

BAR-TAILED GODWIT   Length 14 to 18 in.
Limosa lapponica   Passage migrant and visitor

The Godwit is a large wader, and may be distinguished from others by its superior size and slender, slightly up-curved bill.   It is a bird of passage, and may be seen at any time of the year, but usually in spring and autumn.   The summer plumage is chestnut-red with mottled brown on the upper parts and whitish rump and tail, the latter barred with brown.   In winter the upper parts are greyish, the underparts white.

HAUNT.   The shore and estuaries.

FOOD.   As other waders, and includes sandworms, sandhoppers, shellfish and crustaceans.

NOTES.   Rather harsh and short.

BLACK-TAILED GODWIT Length 16 to 18 in.
Limosa limosa   Passage migrant and visitor

The legs are longer than those of the above, and there is a long, wide, white bar on the dark wing, and black tail with white base and white rump, both seen in flight.   Winter plumage is browner in tone on the back, and in summer it is not so red on the underparts.

Family *SCOLOPACIDAE*

CURLEW   Length 21–23 in.

Numenius arquata   Resident

The Curlew is a strange and attractive bird, with its sad, musical cry and long, curved bill. This call-note is one of the most familiar and heart-stirring sounds of the coast and of the moorlands where the Curlew breeds. It may be heard at night as well as by day as the birds fly overhead. The plumage is brown, beautifully streaked and patterned ; the rump and underparts below the breast are whitish.

HAUNT. Sandy bays, rocky coasts, mud-flats, and the moors where it nests.

NEST. A small quantity of grass or similar material on the ground ; amongst clumps of rushes, grass or ling, on a high moor.

EGGS. 3 or 4, buffish or greenish-yellow, blotched with brown. April and May.

FOOD. Shellfish, sandworms and other sea creatures ; also worms, insects and berries inland.

NOTES. " Curlwee ", and a liquid bubbling note, not so loud. From a distance the usual plaintive call sounds more like " wee, wee ", with a questioning lift at the end of each note.

Family *SCOLOPACIDAE*

WHIMBREL   Length 16 in.

Numenius phaeopus   Chiefly passage migrant

The Whimbrel is a small Curlew, and the plumage is rather similar, though the head is paler, with two deep brown stripes over the crown. The bill is also less long and curved than that of the larger bird. The Whimbrel is a bird of passage, not breeding with us except in N. Scotland, the Shetlands and isles of the north. It is most usually seen in spring or at the end of the summer.

HAUNT. Chiefly the coast, rocky or sandy, and mud-flats.

NEST. A slight hollow in the ground, lined with a little grass or moss.

EGGS. 3 or 4, olive-yellow, blotched with brown. June.

FOOD. Shellfish, crustaceans, tiny rock fish, sand-worms and insects. When breaking its journey across country it eats worms, snails, insects and berries.

NOTES. A rippling titter, and bubbling call at breeding place.

TURNSTONE   Length 9 in.

Arenaria interpres   Chiefly winter visitor

This wader does not breed with us, but it may be seen at all times of year. It is commonest as a winter visitor. The plumage is chestnut and black above, with black on the breast and an odd formation of black bands on the white face and neck. In winter, dull brown above, white beneath with blackish bib. The white on the head is lost. Legs, orange-yellow. Striking black and white bands on tail and wings in flight.

HAUNT. Rocks, seaweedy rockpools and the tide-wrack at the edge of the waves.

FOOD. Sandhoppers, shellfish, crustaceans, etc. As its name implies, it turns over stones in search of food.

NOTES. Usually a short, liquid, thrilling twitter when taking wing. Lovers of the seashore delight in the twitter of small waders and the musical clamour of Oyster-catchers on the shore at night. On a still night on the Cornish coast their piping rises as the tide disturbs the waders, and dies away in the mystery of the dark coast-line.

Family *CHARADRIIDAE*. Plovers.

LAPWING
Vanellus vanellus

Length 12 in.

Resident

The Green Plover, Lapwing, or Pee-wit is a graceful bird when seen on the ground at close quarters, with its fine long crest and glossy iridescent plumage. At a distance the appearance is more black and white. Its heavy rounded wings and flapping flight are characteristic. In winter it may be seen in large numbers on ploughed land, pastures and moors.

HAUNT. Fields, pastures, marshes, tidal mudflats and moors.

NEST. A slight depression in the ground, in a field, pasture or any open place.

EGGS. 4, olive, heavily blotched with very dark brown, pointed at the small end. March–July. Unfortunately the birds are often heartlessly robbed of their eggs, which are considered a dainty.

FOOD. Wireworms, leather jackets, snails, slugs, worms, and all kinds of injurious insects, and their larvae. It is one of our most useful birds.

NOTES. "Peewit", and a long whistling note.

Family *CHARADRIIDAE*.   Plovers

GREY PLOVER   Length 11 in.

Passage migrant and winter visitor

Charadrius squatarola

The Grey or Silver Plover may be seen at any time in the
year, but it is usually a bird of passage and winter visitor.
If it is seen in summer dress the plumage is like that of the
Golden Plover, except that the hood and mantle are mottled
with silver and grey instead of with gold and black; the
underparts are black.   Under the tail and the rump are
whiter, and the tail is barred with white and black.   In
winter dress the plumage is light grey-brown streaked and
spotted, and the underparts below the breast are white.

HAUNT.   Usually the shore.

FOOD.   Like that of other waders, including marine
creatures and insects of the usual kinds.

NOTES.   The notes are high and clear, and at times the
birds call to each other constantly : " tee-oo-ee ".

LITTLE RINGED PLOVER   Length 6 in.

Charadrius dubius   Summer visitor

A rare vagrant now become a summer visitor breeding
chiefly in gravel-pits in home counties.   Very like Ringed
Plover but smaller and without wing-bar, shown in flight.
Bill darker, legs paler.   Flight-note, sharp, high " teeu ".

Family *CHARADRIIDAE*.   Plovers

RINGED PLOVER
Charadrius hiaticula

Length 7½ in.

Resident

This tiny Plover is one of our prettiest waders.   It dashes along the sands by the edge of the sea, with legs twinkling so fast as to become invisible.   After a pause, it runs on again, constantly stopping to pick up titbits.   It is not much afraid of passers-by, but scampers to a safe distance. I have often edged round quietly to observe a party closely. When I came nearer than was to their liking, they took to their wings with a few liquid notes and settled again behind me.   Usually there are several together, and often they are in large mixed flocks of waders, including Sanderlings and Dunlins.   The plumage is light grey-brown above and white beneath, with black bands across the forehead and round the neck.   On the breast is a black gorget, and there is a conspicuous white wing-bar.

HAUNT.   Sandy shores ; sometimes by inland water.

NEST.   A slight depression in a sand or pebble ridge above high water ; or inland.

EGGS.   3 or 4, yellowish, spotted with dark brown. April–June.

FOOD.   Sandworms, hoppers, shellfish, small crustaceans, shrimps, insects.

NOTES.   A delicious, liquid " tooi ", and soft " ooi-ooi-ooi " rippling song.

Family *CHARADRIIDAE*. Plovers

GOLDEN PLOVER

Charadrius apricarius

Length 11 in.

Southern form: Resident
Northern form: Migrant

The summer dress of this Plover is remarkable. It wears a spotted hood and cloak of gold and black with a white border. The cheeks, chin and underparts of the Northern form are black ; of the Southern, dusky with black belly and obscured white border. Winter plumage : black parts become white ; face, breast and flanks speckled brown ; upper parts less golden.

HAUNT. Moors, fields, mud-flats and the shore.

NEST (SOUTHERN FORM). The nest is on the ground on a moor in the north or west of the British Isles. Practically no nesting material is used. The Northern form (subspecies) is only an uncommon migrant and winter visitor here, breeding in Iceland, N. Scandinavia and Russia.

EGGS. 4, buff, heavily blotched with very dark brown, very pointed at the small end. May.

FOOD. On mud-flats it will eat marine invertebrates, as do other waders, and on land it feeds on worms, insects, snails, berries and seeds.

NOTES. Liquid notes : " too-ee " and others rather similar.

DOTTEREL

Charadrius morinellus

Length 8½ in.

May–October

  This little Plover is an uncommon summer visitor and migrant in spring and autumn. A few nest in the Grampians and other high places. It has been much harassed by collectors. It is pathetically tame and unsuspecting, and courageous when with young or eggs, feigning injury to draw attention from the spot. The plumage is better illustrated than described : beautifully marked on head and neck, with chestnut and black on the lower breast.

  H A U N T. High mountain-tops ; on passage, moors or shore.

  N E S T. A slight hollow in the ground.

  E G G S. Buff, spotted with dark brown.

  F O O D. Insects, worms, larvae, shellfish, snails.

  N O T E S. A plaintive pipe, a trill, and other low notes.

KENTISH PLOVER

Charadrius alexandrinus

Length 6¼ in.

Summer visitor

  A very rare summer visitor, nesting only on a small piece of south coast. Smaller than Ringed Plover. Light brown plumage has warmer tone. Underparts white. No black except one little bar on forehead and patches on each side of breast. Female lacks black on plumage. Legs and bill black.

  Haunt, nest, eggs and food like Ringed Plover's.

Family *HAEMATOPODIDAE*

OYSTER CATCHER

Haematopus ostralegus

Length 17 in.

Resident

This handsome bird is typical of the rocky and sandy shore, more common on the west coast than the east. The plumage is glossy black on the head, upper breast and back. A bar on the wing and across the base of the tail, and the underparts, are white. In winter there is a white band across the throat. The long orange-scarlet bill catches the eye.

HAUNT. Rocky coasts and sandy shores.

NEST. The nesting material is generally only a few bits of broken shell, and the nest is in shingle or rocks ; but, rarely, it is in grass near the coast.

EGGS. 3 or 4, yellowish, blotched with dark brown. May.

FOOD. Sandworms, shellfish, crustaceans, tiny fish and shrimps.

NOTES. " Peet, peet ", and a trilling whistle. The usual cry of " peet " or " pic " when heard on a cliff from birds on the rocks below is a pleasant rising and falling clamour. It more resembles " pink-a-pink-a-pink ".

Family *LARIDAE*.   Gulls and Terns

COMMON GULL

Larus canus

Length 16 in.

Resident

The name " Common " is misleading, as in most places the Black-headed Gull is far more abundant, and in some the Herring Gull is commoner.   In size it rather resembles the Black-headed, but may be distinguished, even when the latter is without black on the head, by the colour of the legs and bill.   The bill is greenish-yellow and the legs greyish or yellowish-green.   The plumage is white with a soft grey mantle.   The black wing-tips have white " mirrors ". Immature plumage is mottled with brown.   This gull is chiefly a winter visitor to the south and resident in N. Britain.

H A U N T.   The coast ; and, occasionally, inland waters.

N E S T.   On a moor; or on an island or cliff ledge, in a colony with others.   Materials : dry seaweed and grass.

E G G S.   2 or 3, variable ; olive, buff or greenish-blue, spotted with brown or black.   Occasionally unspotted. May.

F O O D.   Small fish, sandworms, shellfish, crustaceans, carrion and odd scraps of all sorts.   Like other Gulls, it also feeds on land and follows the plough, eating worms, grubs and insects.

N O T E S.   A yelp, and other laughing and chattering cries, like other Gulls.

HERRING GULL

Length 22 in.

Larus argentatus

Resident

This beautiful Gull has a wonderfully strong and graceful flight, often gliding in the teeth of the wind. The plumage is white with soft grey mantle, black wing-tips with white " mirrors ", flesh-pink legs, and yellow bill with a red spot on the lower mandible. Immature plumage is mottled with brown ; the white and grey is not completely gained till the fourth or fifth year.

HAUNT. Coasts ; and occasionally inland.

NEST. A tangle of grass and seaweed on a cliff ledge or grassy side of a sloping cliff.

EGGS. 3, olive, blotched with dark brown. May.

FOOD. Shellfish, sandworms, crustaceans, scraps, carrion, nestlings and eggs. The birds are so fond of scraps that a clamouring flock will always appear and pounce on pieces put out for them, or haunt picnic parties and almost ask for crusts to be thrown. They follow the plough, and grubs, worms and many pests are eaten, and a little grain.

NOTES. Cries, screams and a laughing clamour ; sometimes a dismal whining note, and a quick, low " qua-qua-qua ".

LESSER BLACK-BACKED GULL

Length 21 in.

Larus fuscus   March–October

This Gull is nearest to the Herring Gull in size, but may be distinguished by its very dark mantle, and may be told from the Great Black-back by its much smaller size and by its yellow legs. The bill is also yellow with a red spot on the lower mandible. Most of the plumage is spotless white. The wing-tips are black with white " mirrors ". The immature plumage, mottled with brown, lingers for 3 or 4 years.

HAUNT. The coast. It also frequently goes inland. It is a summer visitor, though a few may winter.

NEST. Usually a certain amount of seaweed and grass, on a sloping, grassy cliff or island, or in a marsh, with other Black-backs.

EGGS. 2 or 3, greenish, olive or buff, spotted with brown. May.

FOOD. It eats small fish and the usual marine animals and carrion ; also seabirds which it kills, and their eggs and young. Inland, grubs, etc., are eaten.

NOTES. It has most of the notes of the Herring Gull, yelping and laughing and wailing.

Family *LARIDAE*. Gulls and Terns.

GREAT BLACK-BACKED GULL

Length 29 in.

Larus marinus   Resident

This is the largest of the Gulls, but not so abundant as most of the others, breeding only in the north and west, as a rule. The flight is wonderfully graceful and strong. It may be told from the Lesser Black-back by its much greater size, and from all other Gulls by the very dark grey (almost black) mantle. The rest of the plumage is snow white, except for black wing-tips with white " mirrors ". The legs are pale flesh-pink, the bill yellow with a red spot on the lower mandible. Brown-spotted, immature plumage is not lost until about the fourth year.

H A U N T.   Coasts and estuaries.

N E S T.   A tangle of seaweed and grass on a rocky isle or cliff ledge.

E G G S.   2 or 3, dark olive or olive-buff, thinly blotched with dark brown. May or June.

F O O D.   Chiefly carrion, and seabirds which it kills, and the eggs and young of any birds. It is a callous murderer, not even eating all it kills.

N O T E S.   Barking notes " agh, agh ", and others.

LITTLE GULL   Length 11 in.

Larus minutus   Mainly a winter visitor

Uncommon autumn and winter visitor. A very small Gull with grey wings without black tips, and red legs. Black on head only in breeding-plumage.   Immature plumage (as in Kittiwake) with black band forming inverted W across wings.

GLAUCOUS GULL   Length 26–32 in.

Larus hyperboreus   Winter visitor

Uncommon winter visitor, as large as Great Black-back, but with light grey mantle and white wing-tips. Rest of plumage also white. Immature plumage only mottled faintly with light brown.

ICELAND GULL   Length 22–26 in.

Larus glaucoides   Winter visitor

Very uncommon winter visitor, like Glaucous Gull, but smaller, slighter, longer-winged (proportionately) and smaller bill.

BLACK-HEADED GULL

Larus ridibundus

Length 15 in.

Resident

This, the smallest of the common Gulls, is easily distinguished when, in spring and summer, it has a dark brown, nearly black, head. At other times it may be confused with the Common Gull, especially as it is actually the commonest of our Gulls on inland waters and the coast. At all times it may be recognised by the deep red bill and legs and the white band along the front edge of the wing. The mantle is very light grey and the black wing-tips are without the usual "mirrors". Young birds are mottled with brown on the wings.

HAUNT. The coast and inland waters.

NEST. Of sticks and grass, etc., in a large colony, usually in a marsh.

EGGS. 2 to 4, bluish-green, olive, buff or brownish, blotched with dark brown. April or May.

FOOD. Scraps and carrion, including waste fish scraps, etc. On land it follows the plough and eats harmful insects and grubs.

NOTES. Various ejaculations and a particularly raucous scream.

KITTIWAKE

Rissa tridactyla

Length 16 in.

Resident

The Kittiwake is a bird of the rocky cliffs and stacks chiefly of the north and west coasts. It may be distinguished from the Black-headed Gull in winter dress and the Common Gull by the plain black wing-tips forming a triangle unspotted by white "mirrors". The Black-headed shows a white band along the front edge of the wing in flight. Other distinguishing points are the nearly black legs and the greenish-yellow bill. The rest of the plumage is white with a soft grey mantle. Immature plumage with black band forming inverted W across wings, and black band across back of neck.

HAUNT. The ocean, coasts, and isles.

NEST. Of grass and seaweed ; in a colony on ledges of steep cliffs.

EGGS. 2 or 3, pale buff or grey, blotched with grey or brown, chiefly in a band round the larger end. May and June.

FOOD. Small fish, crustaceans, etc. Besides surface-feeding, it dives and swims under water after fish.

NOTES. "Kit" and another like "kittiwake" with the stress at the end.

COMMON TERN
Sterna hirundo

Length 14 in.

April–October

The Terns, which are sometimes called " Sea-Swallows ", are dainty birds with long fine lines. They are slighter and smaller than the Gulls. The Common Tern is a summer visitor. The plumage is white, with a very slight grey tinge on the underparts and a soft grey mantle. Crown and nape are black, legs red. The red bill has a black tip. The tail is deeply forked. In autumn the forehead is white, the bill blackish. Immature birds are mottled with buff.

HAUNT. The coast, tidal rivers, or inland.

NEST. A miscellaneous assortment of marine and vegetable oddments ; sometimes practically nothing. The ternery is usually a large colony, and though it may be in a rocky place it is usually on sand-dunes or coastal flats. The largest I know of is a stretch of sandy flats with the nests dotted about so thickly that it is advisable to walk with care.

EGGS. 2 or 3, buff or pale greenish, blotched with dark brown. June.

FOOD. Small fish. Inland, it also catches insects.

NOTES. A sharp " kik " or " kirri ".

SANDWICH TERN
Sterna sandvicensis

Length 16 in.
April–October

The Sandwich Tern is a summer visitor, and may be distinguished from the other Terns by its black legs and feet, and black bill with a yellow tip. It is one of the largest of the family. The white forked tail has shorter streamers than those of the other larger Terns, the crown and nape are black, the mantle soft grey and the underparts white with a very faint suggestion of a pink tinge. In autumn most of the black cap is lost. As with other Terns, immature plumage is mottled.

H A U N T.   Chiefly the coast.

N E S T.   There is no nesting material; the nest is merely a scoop in the sand in which the eggs are laid. The colonies are usually on sand-dunes or shingle.

E G G S.   1 to 3, pale cream or buff, blotched with dark brown. May.

F O O D.   Small fish, for which, like other Terns, it plunges when on the wing.

N O T E S.   " Tre-wit " and others.

Family *LARIDAE*. Gulls and Terns

ARCTIC TERN
Sterna macrura

Length 14½ in.

End April–October

The Arctic Tern closely resembles the Common Tern, though the underparts have a more distinctly grey tone. The mantle is soft grey, the crown and nape black, and the bill and legs red. In autumn the forehead is white, the bill and legs blackish. It is a summer visitor. The breeding haunts are less far south, the terneries being most numerous in Scotland and Ireland.

HAUNT. The coast and occasionally inland.

NEST. Nesting material is slight, and the terneries are on rocky islands or sandy or shingly dunes.

EGGS. 2 or 3, buff or olive, blotched dark brown. June.

FOOD. Small fish.

NOTES. Like those of Common Tern : " krik " or " kee-kee ".

BLACK TERN
Chlidonias niger

Length 9½ in.

Passage migrant

This little Tern, now only a migrant with us, passes in spring and late summer chiefly over south-eastern England, feeding, mostly on insects, over inland waters. The plumage shades softly from slate-grey on tail, back and wings to dark grey on the underparts, deepening to blue-black on the breast, neck and head. Bill and legs are black. In winter : white forehead, neck and underparts ; black crown and nape ; darkish grey wings and tail.

Family *LARIDAE*.   Gulls and Terns

ROSEATE TERN   Length 15 in.
Sterna dougallii   End April–September

   This Roseate Tern is an uncommon summer visitor
to the British Isles. It is never so numerous as the
Common and Arctic Terns, from which it may be
distinguished by the soft pink blush on the underparts and the blackish bill, which is only tinged with
scarlet at the base. The streamers of the long, deeply-
forked tail are longer than those of the Common,
Arctic and Sandwich Terns, though their actual length
is variable. The mantle is light grey, the crown and
nape black, and the legs and feet red. In autumn the
forehead is whitish. The scarceness of this bird is
partly due to collectors and plumage-hunters.
   H A U N T.   The coast.
   N E S T.   The nesting colonies, of which there are
very few, are mostly in rocky places. The nesting
materials are little, or nothing.
   E G G S.   1 or 2, buff, spotted with brown. June.
   F O O D.   Small fish.
   N O T E S.   " Agh " and " qu-it ".

Family *LARIDAE*. Gulls and Terns

LITTLE TERN Length 9½ in.
Sterna albifrons April–End September

   This dainty little bird is a summer visitor. It is the
smallest of our breeding Terns, according to some
authorities well under 10 in. in length. In addition
to its small size, it may be distinguished by its yellow
legs, yellow bill with a black tip and the white on the
forehead, which extends round to above the eye. The
rest of the cap is black, the mantle is soft grey and the
underparts white. The white forked tail has much
shorter streamers than those of the Common, Arctic
and Roseate Terns.

H A U N T. The coast and occasionally inland.

N E S T. There is usually no nesting material.
The small nesting colonies are on sandy flats.

E G G S. 2 to 4, light greyish-buff, with brown and
grey blotches. May or June.

F O O D. Small crustaceans and fish. Near inland
waters it also catches insects.

N O T E S. "Kit, kit", "kirrikirrikirri" and "teeeru".

Family *STERCORARIIDAE*

ARCTIC SKUA
Length 18 in.

Stercorarius parasiticus End April–End October

Summer visitor to extreme north Scotland and N. Isles, breeding in colonies on moors. Also off-shore migrant in autumn on most coasts, especially the east. Plumage in two forms. Light form has creamy-white cheeks, neck and underparts, blackish cap, and dark brown upper parts; dark form is all blackish-brown, except that both forms have whitish patch at base of primaries, seen in flight. Intermediate plumage is also seen. Two central tail-feathers long and pointed in adults. Immatures are all dark, save for wing-patch, with hardly any tail-projection. Chases Terns, etc., until they disgorge fish which it snatches. Other food as Great Skua.

NOTES. Wailing and barking.

GREAT SKUA
Length 23 in.

Stercorarius skua Migrant and summer visitor

Larger than a Herring Gull, heavier, thick-set, with darkish-brown plumage and black bill and legs. Short tail without projection. Conspicuous silvery-white patch at base of primaries. Fish-pirate, chasing other birds even as large as Gannets. Summer visitor Orkneys and Shetlands where it breeds. Off-shore migrant further south in autumn. Besides fish taken from other birds, it eats carrion, eggs, nestlings and smaller birds.

NOTES. Harsh, deep, barking cries and scolding rasp.

PUFFIN
Fratercula arctica

Length 12 in.

Resident

This thickset bird, with its strange, gay-coloured bill, may be found, sometimes in large numbers, round our coasts, chiefly in the west and north. The plumage of the upper parts, crown and a band round the neck is nearly black. The underparts are white, the cheeks grey-white. The feet are bright orange, and the grotesquely massive bill is striped with grey-blue, scarlet and yellow. The Puffin stands in an upright position, like the Razorbills and Guillemots, but it is short and thick-necked in appearance.

HAUNT.   The coast and rocky islets nearby.

NEST.   The nest is in a rabbit burrow or tunnel excavated in the earth by the bird.   Nesting materials are little or none.   The colonies are crowded on a turf-covered island or cliff.

EGGS.   1, nearly white, sometimes with a few rufous or greyish spots.   June.

FOOD.   Fish, for which it dives and swims under water with its wings.

NOTES.   It has several very deep notes.

Family *ALCIDAE*. Auks

RAZORBILL
Alca torda

Length 16 in.

Resident

The Razorbills and the Guillemots are more ocean birds than birds of the coast. They visit our wild rocky stacks and cliffs in the breeding season, but otherwise are not seen on land except when their bodies are washed ashore after a storm, or when they become victims to the waste oil on the sea. It is a sad and common

sight to see dead and dying birds on our shores, with their feathers smeared with black oil.   The plumage is black, with white underparts and white bar on the wing.   There is a white grooved line across the bill. In winter there is white on the cheeks and throat.

HAUNT. The ocean. Resident in British waters.

NEST. There is no nesting material ; the solitary egg is laid on a rocky islet or stack, or a ledge on a precipitous cliff.

EGGS. 1, buffish, nearly white or pale greenish-blue, blotched with dark brown.

FOOD. Fish, for which it dives and swims under water.

NOTES. A grunt or growling note.

GUILLEMOT

Uria aalge

Length 16½ in.

Resident

Like the Razorbill, the Guillemot is more an ocean than a coast bird, remaining at sea except when breeding or storm-driven. It is also a frequent victim of the "oil menace", the bodies of thousands being washed up annually round our shores. Plumage of southern race, very dark grey-brown, with white underparts. In winter there is also white on cheeks and throat. Northern race, breeding on the North Isles and round most of Scottish coast, blackish above.   The "bridled" form (with white eye-ring and thin white line over ear-coverts) occurs in both races, but chiefly in Northern.

H A U N T.   The ocean.   Resident in British waters.

N E S T.   No nest is made; the egg is laid precariously on a ledge of a precipitous stack or cliff.

E G G S.   One disproportionately large pear-shaped egg of any shade of brown, green, yellow or nearly white, with or without blotches or lines of brown.   May.

F O O D.   Fish, for which it dives and swims with its wings under water.

N O T E S.   A deep, harsh, grating note.

Family *ALCIDAE*. Auks

BLACK GUILLEMOT Length about 13½ in.

Cepphus grylle   Resident

This plump little Guillemot of northern coasts is at once distinguished from the more common bird by its small size and very different plumage. In summer dress it is brownish-black, with a very large white patch on the wing. The legs and feet are bright red. The white winter plumage is softly barred with black on the back and head ; the tail is blackish, and so are the wings, except for the large white patch.

HAUNT. It breeds on Irish and N. and N.W. Scottish coasts and the Northern Isles.

NEST. No nesting material is used, the eggs being laid in a crevice in rocks or cliffs.

EGGS. 2, pale cream or greenish-white, blotched with brown and grey. May or June.

FOOD. Crustaceans and fish.

NOTES. A very high, wheezy squeak.

LITTLE AUK   Length 8 in.

Plautus alle   Winter visitor

An irregular winter visitor to our seas. Like a tiny Razor-bill or Guillemot but rounded and short-billed. Gales sometimes drive it ashore.

Family *PROCELLARIIDAE*. Petrels and Shearwaters

STORM PETREL	Length 6 in.
Hydrobates pelagicus	Summer visitor
LEACH'S PETREL	Length 8 in.
Oceanodroma leucorrhoa	Summer visitor

These two Petrels are ocean birds, coming to land only for breeding or when storm-driven. The plumage is brownish-black with white rump and under tail-coverts. Leach's may be told from Storm Petrel by larger size, less black appearance, paler band on central area of wing, forked tail, and bounding, changeful flight. Storm Petrel follows ships with fluttering flight over surface, sometimes pattering on surface with feet.

HAUNT. Storm Petrel breeds on islands off west coasts and North Isles, Leach's only in North Isles.

NEST. Little or no material is used ; the nesting holes may be in turf or crevices in rocks.

EGGS. 1, white, faintly speckled with rufous at the larger end. Leach's, May. Storm, June.

FOOD. Small crustaceans and shellfish, tiny fish, offal and oil ; also sorrel, at the nesting site.

NOTES. Purring, churring and sharper notes.

Family *PROCELLARIIDAE*.   Petrels and
Shearwaters

MANX SHEARWATER   Length 14 in.
Procellaria puffinus   Summer visitor

    This oceanic bird breeds chiefly on islands off the west coasts of the British Isles, but may be seen off most parts of the coast in summer and autumn. The plumage is black above and white beneath. In flight it skims low over the water with straight, stiff wings, " banking " like aircraft.

H A U N T. Usually the sea.

N E S T. It nests in colonies, the nesting-holes being in turf or among rocks. Nesting material is little or none.

E G G S. 1, white. May or June.

F O O D. Small fish, crustaceans, shellfish and squids. On land at the nesting colony it also eats sorrel, as do the Petrels.

N O T E S. It comes to land at breeding places at night, with weird cooing cries and wails, and shuffles to tunnels from which sepulchral, husky voices coo " kuk-kuk-hoo-coo ".

GREAT and SOOTY SHEARWATERS

    Great Shearwater (*Procellaria gravis*), 18 in. Sooty Shearwater (*Procellaria grisea*), 16 in. Uncommon autumn visitors off our coasts. The Great has white upper tail coverts, underparts, and neck, almost to nape. The Sooty is blackish with pale centre to underside of wing.

Family *PROCELLARIIDAE*. Petrels and Shearwaters

FULMAR Length 18½ in.
Fulmarus glacialis Mainly a summer visitor

This northern ocean bird now breeds all round the British Isles except the S.E. coast, and is still spreading and starting new colonies. The plumage is white with a grey mantle and tail and no black. Blue Fulmar (Northern phase) is all blue-grey including head and underparts. In flight it glides with stiff, straight wings and only occasional wing-beats.

HAUNT. The ocean and, at breeding time chiefly, cliffs.

NEST. There is usually no nesting material, the egg being laid on a rocky ledge or in a slight hollow in the turf.

EGGS. 1, white. May.

FOOD. Oily offal and refuse, fish and cuttles.

NOTES. A silent bird except at the colonies, where a low cackling is heard as the birds gape at one another with strange gestures.

Family *GAVIIDAE*. Divers

GREAT NORTHERN DIVER

Length 27–32 in.

Gavia immer

Winter visitor

This beautiful ocean bird visits British seas in winter, and is only occasionally seen in summer, except round the Northern Isles. In summer the upper parts are black with square white spots, the underparts white, the head and neck glossy black, with a band of black and white stripes on the throat. In winter the throat is white, and the upper parts mottled grey. It is the largest species of Diver and its size alone will distinguish it from the Black-throated Diver.

FOOD. Chiefly fish, for which it dives, often remaining under water for several minutes.

NOTES. A grunting or growling note and a wail.

Family *GAVIIDAE*.   Divers

BLACK-THROATED DIVER   Length 25 in.
Gavia arctica   Winter visitor and resident

RED-THROATED DIVER   Length 21–24 in.
Gavia stellata   Winter visitor and resident

These Divers may be dealt with together.   The Red-throated, which is the commoner bird, is a winter visitor to British shores, and also nests in the north of Scotland. Winter plumage is white on the throat and underparts, and the upper parts are brownish-grey, spotted with white. In summer the head and neck are grey, partly striped with white, and there is a large red patch on the throat.   The Black-throated Diver also breeds in north Scotland, but elsewhere it is an uncommon winter visitor.   Winter dress: upper parts grey-brown, underparts white.   (For summer dress see plate.)

HAUNT.   The ocean, and sometimes lochs and inland waters.

NEST.   A little herbage, or nothing ; on the ground near water.

EGGS.   1 or 2, olive-brown, spotted with black.   May or June.

FOOD.   Chiefly fish.

NOTES.   Various notes, including a barking cry and a melancholy shriek or wail.

Family *PODICIPITIDAE*. Grebes

GREAT CRESTED GREBE

Length 19 in.

Podiceps cristatus

Resident

This graceful bird is especially beautiful in spring plumage. The ear-like tufts of the grey crest, and the chestnut and nearly black frill at the base of the head, from which the slender neck emerges, are unmistakable. The upper parts are grey-brown with a chestnut tinge on the flanks, and the underparts are glossy white. In autumn the frill is lost. Immature birds lack tufts and frill, and are grey-brown, striped on the neck. Like other Grebes', the toes are lobed.

HAUNT. Lakes, meres and broads.

NEST. A tangle of floating water-weed and other aquatic vegetation, well out in a mere, or at the edge of the water. The parent covers the eggs with weed before leaving them.

EGGS. 3 or 4, nearly white. April–July.

FOOD. Chiefly fish, also insects, shellfish, tadpoles, etc. The bird dives gracefully and searches for food beneath the surface.

NOTES. Various harsh notes, including a short " jik, jik ", though adult birds are usually rather silent.

Family *PODICIPITIDAE*.   Grebes

BLACK-NECKED GREBE   Length 12 in.

Podiceps nigricollis   Resident, passage migrant
and winter visitor

This Grebe is an uncommon winter visitor, and regular passage migrant ; it breeds in a few localities.   In summer the upper parts are black, with golden plumes on the sides of the head over the ears.   There are no horns or tufts on the crown; the underparts are white.   In winter the head adornments are lost and the white of the underparts extends to the breast and chin.   The general appearance is rather roundabout and small, like the Dabchick.

HAUNT.   Chiefly inland waters.

FOOD.   Water insects, small fish, shellfish, etc., for which it dives, remaining under water for half a minute or much less.

NOTES.   There is a soft call and a clear trilling note.

Family *PODICIPITIDAE*. Grebes

LITTLE GREBE or DABCHICK

Length 10½ in.

Podiceps ruficollis

Resident

The Dabchick is quite a common resident on inland waters. This roundabout, tailless little bird is nearly black in summer, with the cheeks and throat chestnut and the flanks brown. In winter the upper parts are lighter, and the underparts nearly white, including the throat.

HAUNT. Inland waters and estuaries. It is only driven to the coast by hard weather.

NEST. The nest is a floating tangle of water-weeds in a mere or similar haunt, or by the edge of the water.

EGGS. 4 to 6, white. April–June. The parent covers the eggs with weed before leaving them. As with other Grebes, the young chicks climb on to their parents' backs as soon as they take to the water, and snuggle into the back and wing feathers.

FOOD. Chiefly fresh-water insects and shellfish, crustaceans, etc., and small fish.

NOTES. There is a soft call-note and a loud, descending, trilling cry.

Family *PODICIPITIDAE*. Grebes

RED-NECKED GREBE
Podiceps griseigena

Length 17 in.

Winter visitor

This bird is an uncommon visitor, most regular in winter. It is usually a salt-water bird. The plumage of both male and female loses the crest-tufts in winter, and the red on the neck also disappears. At all times of year the back is grey-brown and the underparts white, mottled with pale grey.

HAUNT. Usually the sea, more rarely inland waters.

FOOD. Fish, crustaceans, shellfish and freshwater insects.

SLAVONIAN GREBE
Podiceps auritus

Length 13 in.

Resident

Chiefly a winter visitor, with some resident in north Scotland. The top of the head and upper parts are nearly black, the chin, throat and underparts white, in winter. In summer dress the head and upper neck are black, the back dark brown, the breast and flanks chestnut, the abdomen white ; and the head has a short frill (not so pronounced as that of the Great Crested), and golden " horns " or " ear-tufts ". (For other details, see above.)

Family *RALLIDAE*

WATER RAIL   Length 11 in.
Rallus aquaticus   Resident

The Water Rail is a very secretive bird and most difficult to see, as it is nervous and easily takes fright and conceals itself in rushes or sedges. The plumage is chestnut-brown above, spotted and streaked with black. The face, throat and under-parts are lavender-grey, shading to buff on the abdomen. The flanks are barred with black and white. The bill is red.

HAUNT. Marshes and reed-beds.

NEST. Of sedges, reeds and other vegetation ; in a marsh or other swampy place.

EGGS. 6 to 12, buffish-white or pale brown, spotted with golden-brown and grey. April or May.

FOOD. Insects, worms, tadpoles, spawn, molluscs, berries and seeds.

NOTES. The notes are various, including a soft " chiff " or " whitz" and an explosive scream or groan.

Family *RALLIDAE*

SPOTTED CRAKE
Length 9 in.

Porzana porzana.   Migrant and summer visitor

This is an uncommon passage-migrant, some remaining to nest as summer visitors, and a few staying
to winter. It is much smaller than the Moorhen, but
has the same way of jerking its head rhythmically when
swimming. It is most secretive and difficult to see,
as it usually stays hidden in reeds, and when venturing
forth is quickly alarmed and takes cover. The
plumage is reddish-brown above, streaked with black
and white, and the underparts are paler. The sides
of the head and the breast are greyish, thickly spotted
with white. The bill is yellow with red at the base.

HAUNT. Marshes and swampy places.

NEST. Of rushes, etc., among sedges and reeds.

EGGS. 8 to 12, buff, spotted with dark brown.
May.

FOOD. Insects, worms, molluscs and seeds.

NOTES. Various, including a ticking, Snipe-like
call, and a whip-lash sound, " whit, whit, whit ".

CORNCRAKE or LAND RAIL Length 10½ in.
Crex crex   April–End October

The Corncrake is a summer visitor, and though it is often heard, it is seldom seen, being very secretive in habit, like the other members of this family. It is usually concealed in long grass, and is also semi-nocturnal. The plumage is buff-brown, streaked and spotted with darker brown above and barred on the flanks. A large area of chestnut on the wings catches the eye in flight, and the greyish face has chestnut cheeks.

HAUNT. Long grass and fields grown for hay.

NEST. A slight hollow in the ground, concealed in grass or sedges, and lined with finer grass.

EGGS. 7 to 12, light buff, spotted with red-brown. May and June.

FOOD. Chiefly insects; also slugs, snails, worms and seeds.

NOTES. A harsh " crek, crek ", which may be heard at night as well as by day.

Family *RALLIDAE*

MOORHEN

Gallinula chloropus

Length 13 in.

Resident

The Moorhen, or Waterhen as it is often called, is a very familiar and common bird on all inland water, from the small roadside or farm pond to the large mere or lake. The plumage is nearly black with a white line on the flanks. The white under the tail is conspicuous from behind. The bill is scarlet at the base and yellow at the tip. The bird has a mincing gait, and constantly jerks its tail. When on the water it jerks its head rhythmically as it swims.

HAUNT. Ponds, marshes, lakes and rivers.

NEST. Of rushes and reeds, lined with grass; near water. Sometimes it is in a bush overhanging the water, sometimes on the ground concealed in vegetation, or in a tree.

EGGS. 6 to 12, reddish-buff, spotted with red-brown. April–July.

FOOD. Insects, worms, slugs, berries, seeds and aquatic plants and animals.

NOTES. The ringing squawks and guttural ejaculations of the Moorhen are familiar to most people. " Fullock " is a common one, " chirrick " and " quark ".

COOT   Length 15 in.

Fulica atra   Resident

The Coot is rather like a larger edition of the Moorhen, with a conspicuous white forehead-shield and bill in place of the scarlet bill and shield of the smaller bird. The plumage is grey-black shading to deep black on the neck and head. The toes are lobed with webbing. The bird may be seen in large numbers, but does not frequent little ponds and ditches as does the Moorhen.

H A U N T. Lakes, meres and river-flats. Very hard weather may drive it to the coast.

N E S T. Of flags, reeds, etc.; concealed in aquatic vegetation.

E G G S. 6 to 12, stone-colour, spotted with dark brown or black. April or May.

F O O D. Aquatic plants, freshwater shellfish, grain, worms, etc.

N O T E S. Some of the notes are mellow and ringing, others are sharp and metallic.

Family *COLUMBIDAE.*   Doves and Pigeons

STOCK DOVE   Length 13 in.
Columba oenas   Resident

   The Stock Dove may be distinguished from the
Wood-Pigeon by its much smaller size and the
absence of white on the neck and wings. It is the
same size as the Rock-Dove, but lacks that bird's
white rump and bold wing-bars. The plumage
is grey, paler beneath, with a ruddy tinge on the
breast and a bright green and purple sheen on
the neck, and two short, thin bars at the base of
the wing. Bill yellowish with red base ; feet
deep pink.
   HAUNT. Chiefly open country and cliffs.
   NEST. Usually a hole in a tree, or rocks.
Sometimes in a ruin or creeper or the old nest of
another bird.
   EGGS. 2, creamy-white. March–October.
   FOOD. Chiefly weed-seeds and young shoots ;
also grain, mast, acorns, snails, etc.
   NOTES. A low grunting coo.

Family *COLUMBIDAE*.   Doves and Pigeons

ROCK DOVE

Length 13 in.

Columba livia

Resident

The Rock Dove is the wild forbear of domestic and
" homing " pigeons, and is confined to various places on
the coast.   The plumage is grey with green and purple
sheen on the neck and a whitish rump and lower back.
Two black bars cross the secondaries.   The feet are red.

HAUNT.   Sea cliffs and nearby.

NEST.   Of dry seaweed or twigs and grass ; or a ledge
in a cave or crevice in rocks.

EGGS.   2, white.   March–September.   As with other
Pigeons, the nestlings are fed with milky fluid from the
mother bird's throat.

FOOD.   Weed-seeds, grain, green shoots, snails.

NOTES.   A coo like that of domestic pigeons.

COLLARED DOVE

Length 11 in.

Streptopelia decaocto

Resident

A pale grey Turtle Dove, pink-tinged beneath and
browner above ; black half-collar round back of neck, and
end-half of tail white beneath.   In 1955 spread from
Continent, and now breeds in many parts of Britain.

Family *COLUMBIDAE*.   Doves and Pigeons

RING DOVE or WOOD PIGEON
Length 16 in.

Columba palumbus   Resident

The soft coo of the Wood Pigeon has a soothing and sleepy sound on spring and summer days. The bird may be distinguished from all the other Pigeons or Doves by its much greater size, the white mark on the neck and the large white bar on the wing, which is very noticeable in flight. The general colour of the plumage is grey, lighter beneath and nearly black on the tail. There is a dusky reddish tinge on the breast.   Besides the white bar there is a purple and green sheen on the neck.

HAUNT. Woods, gardens, etc.

NEST. Rather flat, of sticks ; in a tree or bush.

EGGS. 2, white. April–August. Sometimes earlier or later.

FOOD. Weed-seeds, young sprouting green, grain, acorns, nuts, berries, caterpillars and slugs, etc.

NOTES. " Coo-coo-cooo-c-cooo,   cuk ", ending abruptly on the last syllable as if interrupted. A familiar version is " Tak' two coos, Taffy ; tak' two coos, Taffy, tak' ".

Family *COLUMBIDAE*.   Doves and Pigeons

TURTLE DOVE   Length 11 in.
                          End April–Beginning October
Streptopelia turtur

The Turtle Dove is smaller and slimmer than the
other Doves and is the only one which is not resident.
It is a summer visitor, and is most common in England,
being usually only a passage migrant in Scotland.
The plumage is chestnut on the back with black
markings ; the underparts are pinkish, the head,
flanks and rump are light grey, with a few black and
white stripes on the sides of the neck.   The black tail
is wedge-shaped with a bold white border to the tip,
conspicuous in flight.   The legs are red.

HAUNT.   Chiefly rather open, thinly tree-clad
country.

NEST.   A flimsy nest is made of twigs, usually high
in a tree.

EGGS.   2, white.   May or June.

FOOD.   Weed-seeds, young green shoots, grain
and insects.

NOTES.   A soft, purring note.

Family *PHASIANIDAE*.   Pheasants and
Partridges

PARTRIDGE
Perdix perdix

Length 12 in.
Resident

A fat brown game-bird with whirring and gliding flight
and chestnut tail.   It rises suddenly with a loud whirring,
and glides low with arched, stiff wings.   The head is
sandy, neck and breast grey, underparts paler, barred with
chestnut on the flanks and with a horse-shoe-shaped patch
of chocolate on the belly.

HAUNT.   Chiefly cultivated land.

NEST.   A hollow, lined with grass and leaves, concealed
in vegetation under a bush or hedge.

EGGS.   7 to 20, usually 12 to 16, olive.   April–July.

FOOD.   Weed-seeds, caterpillars, insects of all kinds ;
also grain, green shoots and grass.

NOTES.   A distinctive creaking note, " cheevik ".

RED-LEGGED or FRENCH PARTRIDGE
Length 13½ in.

Alectoris rufa

Resident

Chiefly confined to south half of Britain, not including
Cornwall and Devon.   Plentiful in S.E. counties.   Differs
chiefly in white, black-edged cheeks and bib, striking bars
on flanks of black, white and chestnut, and red bill and
legs.   Notes :   " chucker, chucker ", and knife-grinding
sounds.

Family *PHASIANIDAE*. Pheasants and Partridges

QUAIL   Length 7 in.
Coturnix coturnix   End April–October

This plump brown little game bird, rather like a miniature Partridge, is a summer visitor, usually rather scarce, though variable in numbers. Plumage reddish-buff, streaked with cream and black, and mottled with darker brown on the upper parts. Dark stripes on the throat and neck of the male are variable. The throat varies from nearly white to chestnut.

HAUNT. Fields and wastes, where it takes cover in herbage, and generally remains unseen.

NEST. Of grass ; on the ground, concealed in herbage.

EGGS. 7 to 10, buffish, speckled or blotched with brown. May or June.

FOOD. Weed-seeds of all kinds, especially chickweed ; also insects and green shoots.

NOTES. A liquid triple note, something like " wet-we-wit ".

Family *PHASIANIDAE*.   Pheasants and Partridges

PHEASANT

Phasianus colchicus

Length 21–35 in.

Resident

This semi-domestic bird, with its beautiful plumage, is too well known to need minute description. Even those of us who have not seen the living bird at close quarters are familiar with the sight of Pheasants in poulterers' shops. The plumage is chestnut-brown, handsomely marked with cream and black, and with an iridescent sheen of green and purple. Behind the bright red, featherless face are two " ear-tufts ". The hen Pheasant is a quiet and sombre-looking bird with mottled brown plumage and not so long a tail.

HAUNT. Usually woods and thick covert.

NEST. A hollow in the ground, lined with a little grass and leaves, and usually concealed in close covert or a hedge.

EGGS. 7 to 18, usually 10 to 12, pale olive. April–June.

FOOD. Seeds, grubs, insects, ants' eggs, grain, mast, berries and many other animal and vegetable atoms.

NOTES. The loud and startling clatter or crow is well known.

Family *TETRAONIDAE*. Grouse

RED GROUSE
Lagopus lagopus scoticus

Length 15 in.

Resident

This bird of high moorlands is resident in northern England, Scotland, Wales, and Ireland. It flies low with whirring and gliding arched wings. Male : dark, mottled, red-brown with blackish tail and wing-tips and red combs over eyes. Female : smaller and not so dark. Sub-species of Willow Grouse.

NEST. Hollow in the ground in heather or similar shrubby plants.

EGGS. 6 to 14, buff, mottled with brown. April, May.

FOOD. Seeds and berries, of heather and other moorland plants and shrubs, shoots, leaves, caterpillars and other insects.

NOTES. A crow : " kok, kok, kok " and " gobak, gobak, gobak ".

BLACK GROUSE
Lyrurus tetrix

Length 21 in. (Male)

Resident

Resident in north and west Britain on rocky or tree-sprinkled moors, marshes and plantations. Male : glossy black with lyre-shaped tail, white under tail and white wing-bar. Female (16 in.) : mottled brown. Nest, eggs and food as above. Notes. In display at " lek ", gobbling and bubbling.

PTARMIGAN
Lagopus mutus

Length 14 in.
Resident

The Ptarmigan is a bird of high Scottish mountains and a few north-western isles. The plumage in winter is white except for some black on the tail and a black patch from bill to eye of male. In spring there are brown, grey and buff bars on the body-plumage of the male ; the female is more sandy in tone. In autumn the upper parts of the male are grey, and the female is slightly browner. Both birds have a red comb over the eye, but that of the male is more pronounced.

HAUNT. Rocky heights and mountains.

NEST. As a rule no nesting material is used, the eggs being laid in a slight hollow.

EGGS. 7 to 10, buff or yellowish, mottled with brown. June.

FOOD. Berries, seeds, lichens, mosses, green shoots, leaves, etc.

NOTES. A low croaking rattle.

Family *TETRAONIDAE*. Grouse

CAPERCAILLIE
Tetrao urogallus

Length 33 to 35 in. (Male)
Resident

This strange - looking forest bird is most handsome when it parades with spread tail and drooping wings in nuptial display. The plumage is blackish with deep metallic green on the breast, and a brown tinge on the wings, and there is a long, bright - red wattle over the eye. The female, which is only 22 to 25 in. in length, is red-brown, mottled with buff, whitish and black.

HAUNT. Forests and woods in Scotland, chiefly fir forests where it was reintroduced in the early 19th century.

NEST. A hollow in the ground with very little lining.

EGGS. 6 to 10, buff, speckled with chestnut. April or May.

FOOD. Young leaves, shoots and pine needles, berries and insects.

NOTES. Strange notes are heard in nuptial display. Coward says : " Various observers have heard notes which remind them of the squalls of fighting cats, of the drawing of corks, and the sound of grinding knives. The hens gather to listen to the song, answering with excited croaks."

INDEX

218

INDEX

INDEX

INDEX

INDEX

INDEX

PRINTED FOR THE PUBLISHERS BY
WILLIAM CLOWES AND SONS LTD, LONDON AND BECCLES

527.1166